MW00997237

SHADOW & LIGHT

a JOURNEY into ADVENT

TSH OXENREIDER

HARVEST HOUSE PUBLISHERS

Eugene, Oregon

Unless otherwise indicated, all Scripture quotations are taken from the
New Revised Standard Version Bible, copyright © 1989 by the Division of Christian
Education of the National Council of the Churches of Christ in the United States
of America. Used by permission. All rights reserved worldwide.

Verses marked NLT are taken from the Holy Bible, New Living Translation,
copyright © 1996, 2004, 2015 by Tyndale House Foundation. Used by permission of
Tyndale House Publishers, Inc., Carol Stream, Illinois 60188. All rights reserved.

Cover art and interior design by Connie Gabbert Design + Illustration

Published in association with Jenni Burke of Illuminate Literary Agency,
www.illuminateliterary.com

For bulk, special sales, or ministry purchases, please call 1.800.547.8979.
Email: customerservice@hhpbooks.com

Shadow and Light
Copyright © 2020 by Tsh Oxenreider
Published by Harvest House Publishers
Eugene, Oregon 97408
www.harvesthousepublishers.com

ISBN 978-0-7369-8060-9 (Hardcover)
ISBN 978-0-7369-8061-6 (eBook)

Library of Congress Control Number: 2020937192

All rights reserved. No part of this publication may be reproduced,
stored in a retrieval system, or transmitted in any form or by any means—electronic,
mechanical, digital, photocopy, recording, or any other—except for brief
quotations in printed reviews, without the prior permission of the publisher.

Printed in the United States of America

20 21 22 23 24 25 26 27 28 / VP-CG / 10 9 8 7 6 5 4 3 2

CONTENTS

AN INVITATION

Just when everything is bearing down on us to such an extent that we can scarcely withstand it, the Christmas message comes to tell us that all our ideas are wrong, and that what we take to be evil and dark is really good and light because it comes from God. Our eyes are at fault, that is all. God is in the manger, wealth in poverty, light in darkness, succor in abandonment. No evil can befall us; whatever men may do to us, they cannot but serve the God who is secretly revealed as love and rules the world and our lives.

DIETRICH BONHOEFFER[1]

INTRODUCTION

What words, sights, sounds, and smells come to mind when you think of Advent?

Depending on your upbringing, church tradition, culture, and perspective, you might consider Advent a foreign concept (perhaps you've heard of the word, but you're not sure what it means beyond a type of cardboard-cutout calendar you can buy from the holiday aisle at the grocery store), or you might picture a lengthy, 40-day Orthodox season of fasting from meat, dairy, fish, wine, and olive oil before celebrating the beloved Feast of the Nativity on December 25. Many of us probably sit somewhere between these two ideas.

Regardless of your relationship with Advent, you most likely have some kind of relationship with Christmas. It might be your favorite time of year, and you employ all your restraint and willpower to refrain from blasting carols from your speakers in October. Or you might flat-out dread this time of togetherness, tradition, and toasting to indulgence, and you have to muster all your strength to power through it while longing for life to return to "normal." Once more, many of us probably sit somewhere between these two ideas.

No matter your position, Advent is a gift. It's an invitation to move slowly and methodically, looking inward with honesty about your relationship with God

incarnate. It doesn't matter where you begin your Advent journey. What matters is that you're invited.

This book is written as a guide for the journey: intentionally short, ecumenical, and requiring almost no preparation. Many of us don't respond to our invitation to participate in Advent because of busyness, confusion, or overload. This guide aims to remove those barriers, offering a sensory-rich summons to enter the season as we are, wherever we are in life.

Working long, ten-hour shifts five days a week? This invitation is for you. Sleep deprived with small children who have overtaken your house and life? This invitation is for you. Young and immersed in studies with barely enough time to eat? This invitation is for you. In your second half of life, feeling a bit lost on what's beyond the bend? This invitation is for you too.

I first wrote this devotional to meet my own family's needs for an Advent guide that was short but rich with meaning—marinated in tradition, yet fit for a family of laypeople. Because Advent is for all of us. Honoring the season doesn't need to be complicated. It simply requires that we take the first step and respond to the invitation.

Having grown up in a Christian home and attended church regularly, I knew *about* Advent. I'd heard of it, watched someone light a candle every Sunday, and saw the store aisles of cardboard calendars with perforated doors hiding mediocre chocolate. But I never understood what Advent was.

Our nondenominational Southern church traditions were fairly low key and dependent on the mood and whim of our local pastoral leadership. We sang Christmas carols all throughout December, had a Christmas Eve candlelight service, and usually put together some sort of Christmas production for the community—a musical diorama of some form of the Nativity story.

At home, we would participate in our own family traditions, such as movie watching, tree trimming, gift wrapping, baking—the usual for an American family. Christmas Day was a joy-infused, colorful mess of wrapping paper and Andy Williams on the record player, followed by extended family time replete with overeating and more gifts. And then—it was over.

December 26 was always an abrupt letdown, when it felt as if the literal and figurative lights were promptly switched off and the celebrating ceased. Our family managed to keep our outdoor lights lit through January 1, but our tree was usually tossed out on the curb sometime during the last week of the year. By the start of the new year, Christmas was little more than a recent memory, with the adults eager to get back to routine and regularity.

I share this as an explanation of my Advent backstory. For me, *Advent* was simply another word mentioned around December, and it had something to do with lighting a candle at church. As a child, my priorities were more aligned with watching *Rudolph the Red-Nosed Reindeer* on TV. That's not a bad thing, of course. I simply didn't know what Advent was. It was another vague and foreign holiday word, like *frankincense*, *sugarplum*, or *tidings*.

I'm an adult now and a mother of three growing children. My family of five has lived in many different settings, both in the States and abroad, and our holiday traditions varied widely during our family's early years. There isn't one particular thing we have always done the same. Recognizing Advent, however, is the most consistent practice in our familial repertoire, an observance we wholeheartedly and collectively anticipate.

My husband and I were confirmed as Anglicans a while ago; he grew up Baptist, and I was raised in a nondenominational setting. There are whole chapters I could write on what I love about the Anglo-Catholic tradition and about the grace of sacramental theology, but a favorite is observing the traditional Church calendar. The calendar isn't at all unique to Anglicanism. Catholics, as well as several Protestant denominations, have long recognized this same liturgical calendar, and there's been a resurgence of interest among other Christians.

There are shelves of weighty books written about the full liturgical calendar, and this short book isn't meant to replace them. But because Advent is of paramount importance to that calendar, I'll explain the basics in the next section in order to help you better understand how our observance of Advent rests in context with the rest of the year.

I have long loved (and still love) the Christmas season, so even before we became Anglicans, I relished the idea of doing something for Advent as a parent. I loved the childlike idea of stretching out Christmas as long as possible, of being a fun mom who helped cultivate holiday anticipation with crafts and cookies (this was during my early foray into parenthood, when I ignored my innate wiring and denied the basic truth that *crafty* is not a word to describe my style). I truly wanted to recognize the spirit of Advent even though I didn't understand it, and the internet gave me a plethora of ideas—like hanging homemade ornaments on a Jesse tree or following a streamlined Advent calendar with activities I had chosen for daily holiday merrymaking.

These ideas left me exhausted, resentful, and befuddled about the actual purpose of Advent in our life—and therefore eager for the holidays to just end already. My spirit wanted to honor Advent because it would bring more depth and meaning to Christmas, but I couldn't figure out how to "do it" the way that would work best.

Our family eventually shifted to simply lighting Advent candles at home each week, building up to the culmination of Christmas Day, when all five candles would finally glow. This was much better—it felt less pressured, less complicated, and more reverent. Quiet. Reflective. Soulful.

For the sake of our three kids, I wanted each gathering to have meaning—

I didn't want us to light a candle, say, "Well, that's nice," then hear someone ask to pass the butter. So we added a devotional reading to our candle-lighting ritual. We tried quite a few books meant for reading aloud as a family, and some were better than others. But there were two problems: We couldn't find one that rested on a simple but historical and ecumenical explanation of Advent, and the pressure was still too much.

Sometimes our readings were confusing for the younger set, so we would then read a child-oriented book—but those were watered down and belittling. Plus, with our three children spanning five years, each one was in a different developmental stage. What worked for our oldest was over the head of our youngest, and what could have passed for our youngest was eye-roll worthy for our oldest.

I just wanted something simple—something that spoke to me as an adult who longed for an invitation to focus on the incarnation of Christ, and something that spoke to my growing children as well. I wanted something rich, but nothing so theologically dense that it was a slog. And, to be honest, we needed something quick. Our kids have school and extracurricular activities during Advent, so by the end of the day our bodies are tired and our minds are restless. I wanted something steeped in mystery but fuss-free, something that would help us savor the anticipation of Advent as we ended our evenings.

This book is the result of honoring our need to venerate the true season of Advent as separate from Christmastide without complicated cultural pressure or excess activity. It leans heavily on the artistry of others and on the good work of the historic Church mothers and fathers who have already laid the foundation.

Advent has grown in my life from a meaningless holiday word to my favorite liturgical season of the year. My prayer for you is that the words on these pages will give you the freedom you need to dive fully into this blessed season of waiting and anticipation.

THE BASICS OF ADVENT

Before diving into the meat of this Advent guide, let's explore a few whys, whens, and whatnots. What is Advent, really? And how is it not just part of the Christmas season?

THE LITURGICAL YEAR

Liturgy is an invitation for the people of God to participate in the work of God. The liturgical year, therefore, is a recognition and celebration of feasts and seasons, transforming our ordinary 12-month calendar into sacred time. We inherited the idea from our Jewish ancestors in the Old Testament, who commemorated both holy days, such as Yom Kippur, and holy ordinary practices, such as recognizing a sabbath day every one day out of seven. People have marked time and seasons since the beginning of written history, and followers of Christ have continued this ancient Jewish tradition since the early days of the Church.[2]

The Christian liturgical calendar has evolved over time, but it began with the global Church's desire to set aside Sunday as a sabbath day to recognize the resurrection of Christ. The rhythmic seasons in the Church calendar also reflect the natural world's cycles of sowing and reaping. These organic cycles speak to the mystery of birth, growth, death, and resurrection that we recognize in the earthly and divine life of Christ.

There are differences between the Western and Eastern Christian calendars, and this guide is written with the Western calendar in mind, in which the main liturgical seasons progress as follows:

- *Advent*
- *Christmastide*
- *Epiphany*
- *Lent*
- *Holy Week*
- *Eastertide*
- *Ordinary Time*

There are important feast days within these seasons, such as Trinity Sunday and All Saints' Day, as well as specific saints' days, such as Saint Nicholas Day and Saint Patrick's Day, but the liturgical calendar is largely divided into these seven seasons. And like the gospel itself, the calendar revolves around two divine movements: the welcome of the Incarnation, commemorated in the Christmas cycle from Advent through Epiphany, and the victory of the resurrection, remembered in the Easter cycle from Lent through Eastertide. In Ordinary Time, the Church's primary focus is to live out its missional calling in the world and to encourage daily growth in its members.

The overall purpose of the liturgical calendar is to "trace the mystery of salvation and the course of salvation history"[3] and to proclaim this salvation as a redemption of time. We lean into the natural, created rhythms of time and let God use them in our lives for personal growth and communal unity.

WHEN, WHY, WHAT, WHO, WHERE, HOW

When Is Advent?

Advent is the first season in the liturgical year, beginning four Sundays before Christmas and ending on Christmas Eve (which is why it's not always the same length every calendar year). The first day of Advent is the "New Year's Day" of the Christian calendar. For specifics, check page 143 for the dates of the first Sunday of Advent through 2030.

Why Do We Commemorate Advent?

The daily readings in this book will unpack this big idea slowly, from the first Sunday of Advent through Christmas Eve. But to summarize, the word *Advent* comes from the Latin word *adventus*, which means coming or visit. Advent is the season of preparation before Christmas, when we celebrate the human incarnation of Christ.

As we prepare, we remember history's longing for a Messiah before Jesus's birth and what it would have been like to wait and wonder. Advent is also a reminder of our anticipation of the return of Christ, when he will restore the earth to its original state and make right all wrongs. This season is a recognition of the current state of life here on earth, acknowledging the fraught tension of living between the time of the *already* of the first Advent of God and the *not yet* of its full, redemptive completion. Advent is about remembering that Christ has already come to save the world while recognizing that the work of redemption will not be finished until he comes again.

Advent is also a realization of our daily, ongoing preparation—the work of inviting the Holy Spirit into our lives and making room for Christ to do a good work in us. We lean into the reality that though we are saved from death because of the cross, we are still a work in progress.

Much like the way we ready our homes for guests when company is coming, we prepare ourselves. We prepare our homes, yes, by slowly decorating for the great Feast of the Nativity on December 25, but we also prepare our hearts, minds, and souls. Advent is the season of expectancy, preparation, and longing.

What Is Our Posture for Advent?

Remember the childlike feeling of giddy excitement about Christmas's arrival, wondering what was inside the boxes under the tree and drooling at the thought of the table spread? This is an accurate posture for Advent. We recognize Advent because our souls long for the full redemption of the world and because Advent aligns our minds with what we already anticipate: a full feasting with Christ.

As a season of reflection, Advent provides the space and freedom necessary to feel and understand what it means to wait on God. Like a child who needs to eat her vegetables before she has dessert, Advent is wisely designed to help us contemplate what it means to need the presence of God before feasting in it.

Who Can Commemorate Advent?

Because Advent is part of the Church calendar and marks our anticipation of Christmastide—when we remember the Incarnation of Jesus Christ—it follows that recognizing Advent is most common with Christians. But you can recognize and participate in Advent even if you're unsure about what you believe. In fact, Advent is a wonderful time to test out the waters of Christian tradition if you'd earnestly like to learn more about what it means to follow Christ. Advent is for everyone.

Where Can We Recognize Advent?

Catholic churches and some Protestant churches, such as certain Anglican and Lutheran congregations, almost always celebrate the Advent season in their parishes during the four weekly services before Christmas Day. Lately, other churches have also found richness in the celebration, so it's quite possible to see at least an Advent wreath with candles lit somewhere in the sanctuary.

Advent can also be celebrated in the home, which is the purpose of this book: to provide an approachable blueprint for commemorating the season among family and friends or on your own. The visual focus is usually a wreath with four or five candles, typically placed in a gathering area in the home, such as the coffee table, dining table, countertop, or hearth.

How Do We Recognize Advent?

There are as many ways to commemorate Advent as there are Christmas traditions, so there is no one right way. But remembering the focus of Advent—preparation, both inward and outward—I find it most helpful to keep things simple. There's no need to burden ourselves with a laundry list of to-dos at the expense of practicing the acts that remind us of what we're really doing when we recognize Advent. Too many good ideas are overwhelming, and they can keep us from doing anything at all.

This is the main reason this book includes only readings and straightforward practices that are life giving. Less is more when it comes to Advent. It provides space to chew on Scripture readings and the meaning of days as we progress, and it also allows the beauty of art and music to wash over us. Let those who have blessed the Church with their gifts bless you and your home.

Feel free to tweak, add, or omit anything in this book, because again, there is no one right way to *do* Advent. Some years you'll find yourself craving more, and other years you'll be grateful for the grace of doing only that which needs doing.

SUPPLIES NEEDED

I say "supplies needed" rather tongue in cheek, because there's hardly anything truly necessary for Advent. You already have this book, so you don't need anything more unless you want it. You don't even need a Bible, because this book includes all the text for Scripture readings (which is helpful if your hands are full or life is busy). If the only thing you desire for Advent is a daily reading, you're set.

But if you'd like to do a bit more, here are a couple ideas.

Candles and a Wreath

Homemade beeswax Advent candles provide a few minutes of tangible communal participation for your family, and they take about five minutes to make (kits are available that include sheets of dyed beeswax and cotton twine for wicks). The upside is the aesthetics of the candles: natural, rustic, and delightfully ordinary.

The downside is that these homemade candles burn quickly, so by Christmas Day, they're usually puddles. You'll most likely need a new kit every year, so if you prefer candles you can use year after year, you might want to buy long-lasting premade ones.

Wreaths can be made from anything, but there's something decidedly poignant about them when they're crafted from nature. Use twigs and leaves from your backyard, pine boughs cut from your local Christmas tree seller, or a bowl filled with cranberries and pine cones. Our family typically drills five holes into a simple log from a backyard tree. It pairs well with beeswax candles, and there's a symbolic resonance to recognizing Advent with nature as a reminder that all creation waits in anticipation along with us. We keep the log on our coffee table or our dining table as the centerpiece for the season.

You simply need five candles and a place to hold them: one candle for each week of Advent, plus a Christmas candle.

The Meaning Behind the Colors

Advent candles can be any color you like, but purple is the traditional color for the Advent season in the liturgical calendar. (In some traditions, purple is replaced by blue.) This means that most of the season's candles are purple, with an additional pink candle for the third week and a white candle for the Christmas season.

Why these colors? There's not one universally accepted answer, but the most common idea is that purple is the color of both royalty and repentance. This color helps us remember that the coming Christ is the Prince of Peace, but also that we're meant to repent and reflect on the inner state of our souls as he arrives daily in our lives.

But the season isn't all dirge, because the pink candle for the third week symbolizes joy, Advent's minor theme. With this candle, we're asked to remember that even though Advent taps into our yearning for God's nearness, we know he has already drawn near through the incarnate Christ, whose earthly birth we will soon celebrate. Thus, the combination of one pink and three purple candles paints a portrait of Advent's overarching theme: sober anticipation mixed with a hint of joy.

Each candle also has several themes associated with it, none of which are universal in the broader Church. Some traditions say the candles represent, in order, hope, love, joy, and peace. Others say they represent expectation, hope, joy, and purity.

To provide structure for our Advent practice, I look to the uncomplicated weekly meanings of hope, faith, joy, and peace as our scaffolding. I also see the connection between hope and expectation, faith and preparation, joy and anticipation, and peace and gratitude. Therefore, this guide is divided into those four stages: expectation, preparation, anticipation, and gratitude. I find that most of us naturally flow through these emotional rhythms during the holiday season.

In the first week, I'm eager to begin and can't help but come to the table with expectation. I have hope that the following weeks will be full of right focus, and God, in turn, asks for my trust that right hope in the incarnate Christ will not be misplaced.

Sometime around the second week, our family begins to pull the Christmas decorations down from the attic in preparation for feasting in a few weeks' time. I prefer to do this slowly, partly so I don't burn out on garlands and gingerbread before Christmas even begins—but also to symbolize the faith we have in our good God, who provides the world with redemption through Jesus. We can rest in hope that God will meet us in due time with all we need.

By week three, our entire family is eager for the arrival of Christmas. We adults sense a mild panic, but the kids are full of anticipation that the upcoming celebrations will be all that they imagine. The joy, when we remember what we're about to celebrate—the Lord's arrival—is palpable.

Finally, by the last week of Advent, there is gratitude for all that we've experienced in the previous three weeks: goodness as we've walked with God through expectation, preparation, and anticipation. And there's peace about what's to come.

This book helps you walk through Advent as a four-week focus on hope, faith, joy, and peace. Let yourself feel the expectation, preparation, anticipation, and gratitude pulsing through your veins.

Music and Art

There is no shortage of hauntingly beautiful music and artwork, both ancient and modern, to accompany Advent. It's often hard to wade through the deluge of Christmas carols to find the hymns and compositions that dive into the specific Advent notions of anticipation and expectation. So each day's reading in this book includes a suggested song to listen to (or sing, if that's your preference) as you light the candles, pray, and reflect. There have also been many great artists who have captured the themes of Advent visually, so you'll find suggested artwork to explore and appreciate for different days.

Recommended tools for enjoying these works of music and art are listed in the resources section.

ABOUT THE FORMAT

This book comprises a Scripture reading plan based on the *Book of Common Prayer*, an ecumenical, Anglican collection of prayers, liturgies, and catechisms whose origin stretches back to 1549. Many churches still use it as a guidebook for their weekly services, but it's not necessary to be Anglican or Episcopalian to use and find value in this prayer book—it's friendly to Catholics, evangelicals, and all Christians in between.

The *Book of Common Prayer* also includes the comprehensive Daily Office Lectionary, a plan for reading most of the Bible in two years. By using the Lectionary as a personal or familial reading plan, you're joining thousands of Christians around the world who are reading the same passages of Scripture. It's a lovely, historical instrument of Church unification, and as such it's a fitting framework for Advent readings.

The Lectionary provides guidance for daily readings from the Old Testament, Psalms, New Testament, and Gospels. That can indeed be a lot of reading, but in this book we're not going to read from every category for Advent (though you're most definitely welcome to do so on your own).

Psalms is the Old Testament prayer book. Israelites used these sacred songs and poems to express devotion to the Lord, and they remain in regular use today among church traditions of all types. They range in mood from joyous celebration to solemn hymn and bitter protest. The psalms are some of our earliest examples of creative liturgical expression, providing words that God's people can use even today to connect with their Creator through honest, poetic imagination. Because these psalms touch so well on both our common humanity and God's never-changing presence in our lives, we will park mostly on the book of Psalms as our Advent prayer guide.

Though the psalms aren't usually the sole scriptural focus of Advent, there is a richness found in reading them together as we wait with expectation for the coming Messiah. Then, in the final days of Advent, we'll move to different forms of Scripture found throughout the Old and New Testaments (and not specifically prescribed on these dates in the Revised Common Lectionary) to shift our posture from hopeful expectation to ardent anticipation, ready for Christ incarnate.

Each day's reading includes a quiet reflection, which you can read on your own or out loud as a family or community. A Scripture passage follows (or precedes) the devotion, prescribed from the Daily Office Lectionary. The passages from Psalms for the first few weeks are each meant to be used as a collective prayer, a response to the daily reflection. A contemplative question then follows, which you can ask and answer collectively or use for personal prayer or journaling.

Because families are comprised of people of all ages, you can tweak the reading however it best serves you. Though this Advent devotional isn't written specifically for kids alone, consider that your children might benefit from hearing your own honest answers to the daily questions—questions that don't always have simple answers.

At the end of each reading you'll find suggested music and artwork to ponder. You could press the play button for each day's song as you light the candles, then keep it on as a backdrop as you read and discuss the day's reflection. Or you could wait to listen to it in silence to end your devotional time. Depending on your needs, you could even divide up each daily entry to bookend your day, listening to the song and looking at the artwork in the morning, then reading and reflecting in the evening. There's no one right, prescribed way to approach each day's offering.

You could stretch out this time as long as you want, perhaps lingering over a shared meal, or it can be as quick as the last two minutes before bedtime. Because the candles burn quickly, our family lights them as part of our bedtime routine, but you might want to enjoy the candlelight longer and light yours earlier in the day.

Finally, because this book is open-and-go (meaning there's no advanced preparation necessary on your part), simply turn each day to the corresponding day of Advent, read the passage, ask the question, play the music, and reflect on the day's artwork. That's it. If you need to skip a day or two—or even a week—that's fine. The season is busy for many of us. Simply pick up the book again when you're ready, move forward to the current day, and continue reading. You'll never be behind.

ABOUT THE DAYS AND DATES

Days are separated not by specific dates (such as December 12), but by day within the Advent calendar (such as "Week 3, Tuesday"), so that you can use this devotional guide annually. Remember, Advent begins on a different date each year. However, this also means that Advent is never the same length of time, so starting on December 18, readings are listed by date. When December 18 arrives, shift ahead (if needed) to the corresponding reading so that you're going through these entries during the final days of Advent.

If you find this confusing, you might want to refer to the Advent dates section at the end of the book, then pencil in the calendar date on each day's entry to help you keep track of where you are in your reading.

The Scripture readings are mostly taken from the New Revised Standard Version (NRSV) of the Bible, which is fairly easy to read while remaining faithful to the original meaning. This translation serves the devotional, liturgical, and scholarly needs of the broadest possible range of Christian traditions, including both Protestants and Catholics, and using this translation makes this open-and-go guide as ecumenical as possible.

AN ALTERNATIVE TO THE CHOSEN SCRIPTURAL FOCUS

If you prefer to focus your Advent Scripture reading mostly on the story of Christ's birth, instead of the prescribed Lectionary readings from the Psalms—or if you'd like to add further readings to tell the story of the Messiah's arrival—I've included an alternative plan with Gospel readings of Jesus's life on earth, using the New Living Translation (NLT) because it's easy to understand. You can add this to your Advent reading plan or replace the readings from the Psalms. The additional readings are simply dated December 1–25.

ABOUT CHRISTMAS

Advent is a separate season from Christmastide. During Advent, our focus is on inward and outward preparation for the arrival of the incarnate Christ. Christmastide is a different liturgical season that begins with the Feast of the Nativity on December 25—what we commonly know as Christmas. This is a season, not just a day; Christmastide is technically 12 days long (which is the origin of the carol featuring a partridge in a pear tree). Christmas is a true period of feasting!

Sometimes people are hesitant to focus on Advent because they don't want to delay Christmas—they might feel like the holidays already go by so fast that it's hard to withhold Christmas merriment because the season is so delightful. I get this. I really do. And I have a two-part answer.

First, I'm personally not a cultural purist with Advent. And second, acknowledging Christmastide means that instead of feeling disappointed on December 26, as though the festivities are now over, we can keep celebrating—all the way to January 6, when the season of Epiphany then begins in most cultures. This is a welcome relief to those who want more of Christmas, not less!

Western culture often recognizes the Christmas season as beginning the day after American Thanksgiving and lasting through December 25. This makes it difficult not to sing along to carols playing at the coffee shop, toast with your coworkers during your office Christmas party in early December, or drive around looking at lights in your neighborhood with hot cocoa. It's fun! This is why I say "grace upon grace upon grace" during the Advent season. There's no reason to be a purist and expect the culture around us to bend to our liturgical whims.

Ease into Christmas through Advent in your own home and inwardly in your mind and soul, but enjoy the holiday season with your community. No big deal. Keep in mind that your purpose in observing Advent is to draw near to God's heart for redeeming the world, not to earn points with God for avoiding cultural Christmas affairs.

Because Christmastide is 12 days long, our family keeps the decorations up in our home until January 6, and it's in these weeks that we feast, enjoy as many Christmas movies as we can stand, and generally make merry by delaying the end of the holiday until it historically ends. Again, we're not purists, and we don't tackle our non-liturgical friends to the ground when they start taking down their trees on December 26. We simply enjoy Christmas our way in our home and avoid the nagging feeling that it's "too late" according to cultural standards.

There are several saints' days that fall during the season of Advent—but for the sake of simplicity, I'll only mention the two most well known: Saint Nicholas Day, December 6, and Saint Lucia Day, December 13.

Saint Nicholas Day

The life and legend of Saint Nicholas, as is commonly known, is the origin story of our modern-day Santa Claus. He was born in the third century in the village of Patara, in modern-day southern Turkey. His parents were wealthy, but they died while he was young. He supposedly spent his inheritance helping the sick and poor in his village and eventually was made bishop of the town of Myra. He lived during the reign of the Roman emperor Diocletian, known for his persecution of Christians. Nicholas was imprisoned at some point of his service, but he was also present at the Council of Nicaea.

Nicholas was known for his generosity in the name of Christ by sharing his wealth among those who needed it most. The most well-known legend of his service involves three poor sisters who had no dowry, which meant they were unable to marry (and, in fact, could possibly be sold into slavery, as was the custom in those days). One morning, the family woke to three bags of gold mysteriously waiting for them in their home—dowries for the girls. Some versions of the story say that Nicholas tossed the bags of gold into their window at night so as to remain anonymous (with the gold landing in socks or shoes drying by the fireplace).

I love celebrating the example of the historic Saint Nicholas and his symbol of generosity during the holiday season. Learning about his life also helps answer children's questions about what Santa Claus has to do with Jesus and Christmas: Saint Nicholas was a Christian and loved giving in the name of Christ. We, too, do this on Christmas.

Adding a day to honor Nicholas on December 6, during Advent, adds to our expectant hope. This guide includes an additional Saint Nicholas Day reading for

December 6 in the back, if you'd like to use it to replace that day's regular Advent reading. In addition, many cultures have Saint Nicholas Day traditions, but if you don't live immersed in such a culture, there are a few simple things you could do.

The evening of December 5, our kids leave their shoes outside the front door (or if it's cold, inside by the door). We'll then read a book about the historic Saint Nicholas for story time before bed, then proceed with our Advent reading. In the morning, the kids find a few chocolate coins wrapped in gold foil in their shoes.

As a family, we also like to give a few dollars anonymously on this day, to pay homage to Saint Nicholas's reminder to give generously without a need for recognition. Some years, we ask our church for the name of a family who could use a little extra cash, then we put $20 in their mailbox with a typed note saying we love them and are thinking of them. Other years, we dine out and leave a generous tip for our server (doing our best to leave the restaurant as fast as possible!). Sometimes, we'll donate to a charity we like.

These ideas serve as simple, tangible reminders of the real Saint Nicholas and how he is worthy of emulation. But if recognizing his feast day feels overwhelming, release any burden to do so. Advent is still very much Advent with nothing more than a simple remembrance of Nicholas's life.

Saint Lucia Day

Lesser known than Saint Nicholas Day in much of the Western world, Saint Lucia Day recognizes the life of Lucia of Syracuse. Also known as Saint Lucy, she lived during the reign of the emperor Diocletian, like Saint Nicholas. We don't know much about her, but she supposedly consecrated her life to God by vowing never to marry and instead to donate her dowry to the poor.

When news reached Lucia's betrothed that she planned to give away her dowry and refused to marry, she was ultimately sentenced to a life of prostitution.

The guards came to retrieve her, but legend says they couldn't move her, so they heaped wood on her and set it on fire—but she wouldn't burn. They finally sliced through her neck with a sword.

Because legend also says she was blinded by those soldiers—and she previously wore candles to see in the cavernous dark when she brought provisions to Christians hiding in the catacombs—Lucia is connected to light. Thus, she is honored on one of the darkest days of the year, which reminds us that God pierces dark with light.

This guide includes an additional reading for Saint Lucia Day in the back, should you want to read it on December 13 instead of that day's Advent excerpt. In addition, you could recognize her day in your home like other cultures' traditions around the world, even if it's not common in your area.

In celebration of Saint Lucia Day, the eldest girl wears a wreath-crown with (electric) candles and wakes up the family with breakfast—usually a pastry of some sort. Her rising before the break of day and summoning the family to do the same symbolizes the arrival of light to earth: both in nature, as the northern hemisphere soon reaches its darkest night and begins the turn toward light, and spiritually, with eternal light coming through the incarnate Christ.

SHADOW AND LIGHT

For those in the northern hemisphere, Advent begins in a season of ever-growing dusk, creeping toward the shortest and darkest day of the year. In a time of cooler temperatures and grayer skies, there's a glad welcome when the invitation comes to shift our focus to a new beginning: an arrival.

Jesus of Nazareth arrived in a world of poverty. Born to parents of no renown and raised in a town known for nothing good coming from it (John 1:46), God incarnate made his way from the right hand of the Father into a common world rife with political unrest and injustice. He cloaked himself as a person of insignificance, where very few people knew his true identity.

When the angel Gabriel visited Mary, she lived in a world of shadows. Her betrothed, Joseph, made ends meet as a carpenter, quite possibly *barely* making ends meet because of the outrageous taxation from the imperialist Roman government. Herod the Great's bloody, paranoid reign demanded tactics of mass terror and widespread surveillance. (It really is a wonder that God brought the world's Savior into this time and place in history.)

A young woman who became pregnant out of wedlock in this ancient Jewish culture would have been terrified. But God's promise to Mary wasn't stability or security. His promise, as given through Gabriel, was that the power of the Most High would overshadow her (Luke 1:35).

God redeems darkness. He wants to infiltrate the shadows the hardest life has to offer and bring light beyond our comprehension.

We begin Advent aware of the shadows in our world, big and small. Yet, over the weeks we slowly move toward the light of the world. The candles we light every evening remind us of the impending arrival of our good gift from God, given to all of us more than 2,000 years ago. Those candles also remind us of the hope yet to come, when Christ returns to fully redeem the world.

Advent is pregnant with anticipated arrival. Advent acknowledges shadows and dims them with burgeoning light. So we wait in expectation for the full, radiant, overwhelming light to one day wipe out all darkness forever. This is the hope of Advent.

HELPFUL RESOURCES

You don't need any special supplies to commemorate Advent. But if you'd like to participate in the season beyond reading the devotions and Scripture passages in this book, here are a few recommended resources you might find helpful. Links to preferred sources for supplies, as well as to recommended music and art, can be found at shadowandlightadvent.com.

- *candles: four purple or blue, one pink, and one white*
- *tabletop candleholder(s): a wreath, log, jars, or candlesticks*
- *music streaming service, to play the daily recommended music (under each day's "Listen" section)—you could use the accompanying playlist that includes all the songs, found on the website*
- *internet-enabled sound-streaming system, such as a Bluetooth speaker or a phone or computer*
- *device for viewing the daily recommended artwork (under each day's "Reflect" section) on the internet, such as a phone, tablet, or computer*
- Book of Common Prayer, *if you'd like to dive into more of the readings suggested in the Daily Office Lectionary*

PART 2

THE JOURNEY

*Advent comes, relentlessly and throughout life, with its words
of hope and faith—shepherds and magi, crib and star, Emmanuel and
glory—and stirs our hearts to pinnacles of possibility one more time...
The real Christmas gift, for which Advent is the process, is learning
to hum hope, learning to dance the divine.*

JOAN CHITTISTER[4]

EXPECTATION

One of the essential paradoxes of Advent: that while we wait for God, we are with God all along, that while we need to be reassured of God's arrival, of the arrival of our homecoming, we are already at home. While we wait, we have to trust, to have faith, but it is God's grace that gives us that faith. As with all spiritual knowledge, two things are true, and equally true, at once. The mind can't grasp paradox; it's the knowledge of the soul.

MICHELLE BLAKE[5]

SUNDAY

Light the first purple or blue candle.

Read:

Advent means "arrival," and it speaks of a beginning—*the* beginning. Not only is the start of Advent the first day of the liturgical calendar, and thus a "New Year's Day" for Christians, but it also assumes the arrival of something—or someone. Advent is more than counting down the days until Christmas with paper cutout doors revealing chocolate, biding time until most children's favorite day of the year finally dawns. Like someone anticipating the arrival of a dinner guest, we are invited into the rhythm of Advent to prepare. We do more than impatiently drum our fingers on the table until we're allowed to open gifts under the tree. We prepare ourselves.

Similar to our culture's view of the first day of January as an invitation to reinvent ourselves, Advent gives us the chance to transform our lives—but in small, much more significant ways than a new workout regimen or a less cluttered closet. We are offered the chance to pause the push of holiday merriment and slowly inch away from the shadows. This is a small but significant cultural resistance we can practice in our homes, minds, emotions, and relationships.

Today marks the arrival of Advent—and soon enough, we'll mark the arrival of the Christ child. For now, we revel in this invitation. First, we prepare inwardly.

Pray Psalm 147:1-5,8-9.

Praise the LORD!

34

How good it is to sing praises to our God;

for he is gracious, and a song of praise is fitting.

The LORD builds up Jerusalem;

he gathers the outcasts of Israel.

He heals the brokenhearted,

and binds up their wounds.

He determines the number of the stars;

he gives to all of them their names.

Great is our Lord, and abundant in power;

his understanding is beyond measure...

He covers the heavens with clouds,

prepares rain for the earth,

makes grass grow on the hills.

He gives to the animals their food,

and to the young ravens when they cry.

The word of the Lord. Thanks be to God.

ASK:

What is your honest hope for this Advent season?

LISTEN:

"Praise to the Lord, the Almighty" ("*Lobe den Herren*") by Joachim Neander

REFLECT:

When Dark Gives Way to Light (2018) by Meena Matocha

MONDAY

Light the first purple or blue candle.

Read:

God takes 40 weeks to create a human life in the incubator of a mother's body. As the tendons are woven around the joints and the lungs find strength to eventually breathe air, the parents wait with anticipation to meet their new child: choosing a name, stocking up on supplies, and reading about what to expect in those first sleepless months of parenthood. It is a grace from God that their journey takes the better part of a year.

So, too, grace is in Advent, a season pregnant with the purpose of intentional delay. More than 2,000 years after the historic event of Jesus's birth, we live in a world where Christ already lived. But we still wait until all things will be fully redeemed and made new. The world is not as it should be. Not yet. We wait in the shadows for God's full redemption and perfect light that are promised.

Advent is a small, annual remembrance of our greater waiting for the complete fulfillment of Christ's life on earth: that the world might be redeemed. In this season, as we wait for Christmas, we also wait with an even greater hope for the earth.

Pray Psalm 4:5-8.

Offer right sacrifices,

and put your trust in the LORD.

There are many who say, "O that we might see some good!

Let the light of your face shine on us, O LORD!"

You have put gladness in my heart
more than when their grain and wine abound.
I will both lie down and sleep in peace;
*for you alone, O L*ORD*, make me lie down in safety.*
The word of the Lord. Thanks be to God.

ASK:

When has God shown faithfulness to you in your past?

LISTEN:

"O Come, O Come, Emmanuel" (original source unknown)

REFLECT:

Jesus Hears Mary's Song (2018) by Mike Moyers

TUESDAY

Light the first purple or blue candle.

Read:

The holiday season feels darker, heavier, and harder for those truly oppressed by circumstances that otherwise serve as sound bites for everyone else. We might know an orphan or widow, or we might know of someone who has experienced the disadvantages and loneliness of single parenthood, economic poverty, immigrant status, a taxing job, or having family living thousands of miles away.

In this first week of Advent, note the psalmist's words that God does, indeed, bring justice to the oppressed and strength to their hearts—and he often does this through other people. We can be those people. We can be a match to light a candle of hope for a neighbor this Advent season. Prayerfully consider whom that might be in your life and how you might be an instrument to help bring about God's justice on a darkening earth.

Pray Psalm 10:1-2,10-18.

Why, O LORD, do you stand far off?
Why do you hide yourself in times of trouble?
In arrogance the wicked persecute the poor—
let them be caught in the schemes they have devised…
They stoop, they crouch,
and the helpless fall by their might.
They think in their heart, "God has forgotten,

he has hidden his face, he will never see it."

Rise up, O Lord; O God, lift up your hand;

do not forget the oppressed.

Why do the wicked renounce God,

and say in their hearts, "You will not call us to account"?

But you do see! Indeed you note trouble and grief,

that you may take it into your hands;

the helpless commit themselves to you;

you have been the helper of the orphan.

Break the arm of the wicked and evildoers;

seek out their wickedness until you find none.

The Lord is king forever and ever;

the nations shall perish from his land.

O Lord, you will hear the desire of the meek;

you will strengthen their heart, you will incline your ear

to do justice for the orphan and the oppressed,

so that those from earth may strike terror no more.

The word of the Lord. Thanks be to God.

ASK:

In what way might God remember the oppressed through you this Advent?

LISTEN:

"In Labor All Creation Groans" by Delores Dufner

REFLECT:

The Christ of the Breadlines (1950) by Fritz Eichenberg

WEDNESDAY

Light the first purple or blue candle.

Read:

It is not a coincidence that most children squirm with anticipation and delight at the thought of Christmas's arrival. Little else rivals the joy of the day, especially when it's marked by the epitome of childhood pleasures: new gifts, sugary edibles, and permission to make a mess. Something hardwired in us craves relief from the pressures of life's daily liturgies.

But as a delectable dessert is better savored after a meal of vegetables, so, too, is the delight of Christmas after the delay given to us through Advent. There is wisdom here in this time-honored season, because it asks us to deny our knee-jerk reaction to rush toward the relief of celebration. What a gift it is to take all the time we need to prepare inwardly for the arrival of Christ!

Pray Psalm 119:17-20,24.
Deal bountifully with your servant,
so that I may live and observe your word.
Open my eyes, so that I may behold
wondrous things out of your law.
I live as an alien in the land;
do not hide your commandments from me.
My soul is consumed with longing
for your ordinances at all times...

Your decrees are my delight,

they are my counselors.

The word of the Lord. Thanks be to God.

ASK:

What are you looking forward to about Christmas?

LISTEN:

"Savior of the Nations, Come" by Saint Ambrose

REFLECT:

The Shepherds Went to See the Baby (1998) by Dinah Roe Kendall

THURSDAY

Light the first purple or blue candle.

Read:

When we start driving a new-to-us car, it isn't long before it seems like the make and model of our car has multiplied. We see it everywhere—in parking lots across from our spot and in traffic jams the next lane over. We are made aware of our car's existence elsewhere in our surroundings; we see it where we didn't see it before.

When we reflect at daybreak on a small portion of God's truth, beauty, or goodness, we open ourselves to seeing it unfold in the flesh through a candid comment from a child, a hint of snowfall in the scent of morning air, or the kindness in the smile of our mail carrier. Noticing God helps us *keep* noticing him.

As we move toward the end of the first week of Advent, we move a bit closer toward the season of Christmas. But still, we wait with expectation in the shadows. We remember the glimmer of hope and the steady hand that holds the good lantern. God is with us as we wait.

Pray Psalm 18:25-28,30-33.
With the loyal you show yourself loyal;
with the blameless you show yourself blameless;
with the pure you show yourself pure;
and with the crooked you show yourself perverse.

For you deliver a humble people,
but the haughty eyes you bring down.
It is you who light my lamp;
*the L*ORD*, my God, lights up my darkness...*
This God—his way is perfect;
*the promise of the L*ORD *proves true;*
he is a shield for all who take refuge in him.
*For who is God except the L*ORD*?*
And who is a rock besides our God?—
the God who girded me with strength,
and made my way safe.
He made my feet like the feet of a deer,
and set me secure on the heights.
The word of the Lord. Thanks be to God.

ASK:

Where have you noticed God today?

LISTEN:

"May You Find a Light" by John Arndt and David Gungor

REFLECT:

The Annunciation (1616), by Jacques Bellange

FRIDAY

Light the first purple or blue candle.

Read:

It's easy to see the shadows of earth; our human condition wires us to notice the depraved injustices, the depressing news, the distraught people around us. Because we live in a time of already-but-not-yet, our world is not as it should be. And so we wait, wondering if there is reason to hope.

Shadows imply light. Plato once told the story of a cave of shadows and people entranced by their flickering dance on the wall—yet the shadows are not the reality. They merely hint at the full truth behind those gazing at the wall. We too tend to stare at the shadows in front of us, ignoring the light behind.

If we live in the shadowlands of burden and challenge, our survival depends on the hope that there is a light source and that the shadows weaken the closer we move toward the light. In Advent, then, we recognize the shadows for what they are as we move slowly toward the origin of that ray of light beaming on our cave wall.

Pray Psalm 16:5-11.

The LORD is my chosen portion and my cup;
you hold my lot.
The boundary lines have fallen for me in pleasant places;
I have a goodly heritage.
I bless the LORD who gives me counsel;

in the night also my heart instructs me.
*I keep the L*ord *always before me;*
because he is at my right hand, I shall not be moved.
Therefore my heart is glad, and my soul rejoices;
my body also rests secure.
For you do not give me up to Sheol,
or let your faithful one see the Pit.
You show me the path of life.
In your presence there is fullness of joy;
in your right hand are pleasures forevermore.
The word of the Lord. Thanks be to God.

ASK:

Where do you see the hand of God working in the midst of shadows?

LISTEN:

"Of the Father's Love Begotten" by Aurelius Clemens Prudentius

REFLECT:

José y Maria (2014) by Everett Patterson

SATURDAY

Light the first purple or blue candle.

Read:

God's faithfulness to humanity has persisted throughout time in our recorded history, and it will endure further than our minds can comprehend. As we move forward in the shadows of Advent, slowly aware of God's movement in our own neighborhood, we see that the entire world is invited to adore its King.

The apostle Paul quotes Psalm 117, the shortest psalm in Scripture, to the bourgeoning church in Rome (Romans 15:11), reminding the faithful there to welcome all who want to know God through Christ, be they Jew or Gentile. As the first week of Advent ends and we light only the first candle for the final time, remember the goodness of Christ's light: that when he was born, he illuminated all corners of the world with his earthly presence. As one amalgam of humanity, we can join through time and space to praise God's great, steadfast love—even through the small flicker of candlelight in our home.

Enjoy the expectation of what's to come.

Pray Psalm 117.
*Praise the L*ORD*, all you nations!*
Extol him, all you peoples!
For great is his steadfast love toward us,
*and the faithfulness of the L*ORD *endures forever.*
*Praise the L*ORD*!*

The word of the Lord. Thanks be to God.

ASK:

In what ways have you enjoyed the season of Advent this week?

LISTEN:

"Come, Thou Fount of Every Blessing" by Robert Robinson

REFLECT:

Mary and Joseph Look with Faith on the Child Jesus at His Nativity (1995)
by Elizabeth Wang

PREPARATION

*A celebration of Christ's birth with a sense of adoration,
love, and gratitude toward the God who loved us even to the folly
of giving us his own Son, will be to arrange our life so that
the peace that only God can give may brighten it like a sun.*

ÓSCAR ROMERO[6]

SUNDAY

Light the first purple or blue candle,
then the second purple or blue candle.

Read:

This past week, we recognized our hope with expectation. Hope is hope *because* of faith, because of a trust that believes something good is on the horizon. Light is on the way.

By the second week of Advent, you've most likely already been bombarded with invitations to Christmas revelry. These aren't inherently bad—in fact, these rituals might be some of your most anticipated traditions. But they can jar you from your slow, Advent-driven path toward Christmastide as you participate in communion with the global Church in awareness of your desperate need for light. The colorful strings of lights ask us to celebrate too soon, before we're ready.

Advent is a gift that invites us to slow down and understand why we celebrate. This crawl to Christmastide sets a table before us. The upcoming feast day waits for us with a bounty we will enjoy soon enough.

Say yes to the party invitation. Bake the cookies and send them to the school fundraiser. Order the holiday gifts on your list. But continue to light that dim candle in the dark and remember that the time is coming soon enough for full revelry.

Pray Psalm 148:1-5, 9-12.

Praise the Lord!

Praise the Lord from the heavens;

praise him in the heights!

Praise him, all his angels;

praise him, all his host!

Praise him, sun and moon;

praise him, all you shining stars!

Praise him, you highest heavens,

and you waters above the heavens!

Let them praise the name of the Lord,

for he commanded and they were created...

Mountains and all hills,

fruit trees and all cedars!

Wild animals and all cattle,

creeping things and flying birds!

Kings of the earth and all peoples,

princes and all rulers of the earth!

Young men and women alike,

old and young together!

The word of the Lord. Thanks be to God.

ASK:

What is your honest hope for this second week of Advent?

LISTEN:

"All Things New" by Andy Gullahorn, Andrew Peterson, and Ben Shive

REFLECT:

The Birth of Christ (1405) by Andrei Rublev

MONDAY

Light the first purple or blue candle,
then the second purple or blue candle.

Read:

It's often easy in our modern culture to forget the natural world upon which we've built our skyscrapers and strip malls, highways and impeccably safe playgrounds. But it's there. The natural world is always there, quietly—and sometimes not so quietly—calling out praise to its Creator. It can't help itself.

Dante Alighieri's purported observation is succinct and accurate: "Nature is the art of God." When we admire a painting, we're doing more than applauding the artist's wielding of the brush or choice of color; we're also reflecting on the meaning, message, and purpose of their work. We ask, "What is the artist conveying with this piece?" We can reflect on the same when we contemplate God's artwork—nature itself. What is God conveying with this falling yellowed leaf, this first snowflake of winter, this bark on the tree, this call of the loon?

As you move further into the second week of Advent, from darkness to light, notice how you're keener to see the outlines of shadows. As God speaks to you during this waiting season before Christmas, slow down and notice small fragments of the natural world around you—and ask God, the artist, for the deeper meaning behind the artwork.

Pray Psalm 9:1-2,9-11.

*I will give thanks to the L*ORD *with my whole heart;*
I will tell of all your wonderful deeds.
I will be glad and exult in you;
I will sing praise to your name, O Most High...
*The L*ORD *is a stronghold for the oppressed,*
a stronghold in times of trouble.
And those who know your name put their trust in you,
*for you, O L*ORD, *have not forsaken those who seek you.*
*Sing praises to the L*ORD, *who dwells in Zion.*
Declare his deeds among the peoples.
The word of the Lord. Thanks be to God.

ASK:

What are some examples of God's beauty that you've seen today?

LISTEN:

"The Maker of the Sun and Moon" by Laurence Housman

REFLECT:

Winter Landscape (early twentieth century) by Konstantin Korovin

TUESDAY

Light the first purple or blue candle,
then the second purple or blue candle.

Read:

Currently, the average life span for men and women in the developed world rests somewhere around the late seventies to early eighties, which means most of us can assume we'll have a fairly lengthy life. But if we zoom out to span the breadth of human history on earth, we're barely a blip on the radar—we inhale and exhale, and then we're done before the world has a chance to shift.

This might seem like a perspective that is antithetical to holiday merriment, but reflecting on life's brevity adds to the season's sweetness and its urgency. Remembering that Advent lasts for only the four weeks before Christmas, and Christmastide lasts only twelve days, is strangely similar to how we experience the joys of life: We blink, and they fly by.

God reminds us to measure our days because our lives are mere breaths, simple shadows in the full light of eternity. For what do we wait? In what do we hope? God, and God alone. He is the only reliable foundation on which our cursory lives can depend.

Pray Psalm 39:4-7.
LORD, let me know my end,
and what is the measure of my days;
let me know how fleeting my life is.

You have made my days a few handbreadths,
and my lifetime is as nothing in your sight.
Surely everyone stands as a mere breath. Selah
Surely everyone goes about like a shadow...
And now, O Lord, what do I wait for?
My hope is in you.
The word of the Lord. Thanks be to God.

ASK:

How does remembering the brevity of your life add richness to Advent?

LISTEN:

"Come, Thou Long Expected Jesus" by Charles Wesley

REFLECT:

Nativity (1998) by Hiroshi Tabata

WEDNESDAY

Light the first purple or blue candle,
then the second purple or blue candle.

Read:

By now, your home may be festooned with your holiday decorations (or maybe you're just getting started). Perhaps you've got your set-in-stone collection of family favorites, like the Popsicle-stick ornaments from elementary school and Santa's cotton-ball beard adorning the fridge. Maybe you enjoy the creativity of annually bedecking your home with new garnishes and trimmings.

No matter where you rest on this spectrum, it is probable that your home doesn't reflect your ideal. Our preference for magazine-worthy landscapes fails in light of our economic and bustling reality, and a mere scroll through the internet can leave us feeling like we've fallen short.

It's not wrong to delight in beautiful things, but keeping attuned to life's true and good requires an intentional turning of our eyes. We need God's help to remember the true beauty in the world, because we are so easily distracted by self-serving vanities. The beauty worth lauding during Advent is the slow turning from shadow to light as we inch closer to the celebration of the birth of the Christ child, the hope of all humankind. More than 2,000 years ago, God bedecked the world with hope for countless generations of people. This is the way of the Lord. This is the true beauty of Advent.

Pray Psalm 119:33-37.

Teach me, O Lord, the way of your statutes,
and I will observe it to the end.
Give me understanding, that I may keep your law
and observe it with my whole heart.
Lead me in the path of your commandments,
for I delight in it.
Turn my heart to your decrees,
and not to selfish gain.
Turn my eyes from looking at vanities;
give me life in your ways.

The word of the Lord. Thanks be to God.

ASK:

In what small way have you seen the true beauty of Advent today?

LISTEN:

"Canticle of the Turning" by Rory Cooney

REFLECT:

The Nativity of Christ (2006) by Alyona Knyazeva

THURSDAY

Light the first purple or blue candle,
then the second purple or blue candle.

Read:

We prepare our private homes and personal hearts during Advent for an inward journey from shadow to light, but none of us lives in a vacuum—and most likely, none of us lives terribly far from other people. We prepare for reasons far beyond ourselves and our own needs: We prepare in order to bring Advent to others.

There's no need to look far to bless our neighbors. Yes, it's good to care about the world, but sometimes it feels safer, less messy, and quicker, to give money to a faraway cause than to invite the neighbor down the street over for dinner. There are reasons aplenty: *I don't know her well. He's probably busy. The house is a mess. I'm not a good cook.* In the next day or two, though, move beyond yourself and do it anyway.

Breaking bread—or takeout—over the table is a low-barrier way to grow from acquaintances to friends and to make time for what matters: people. We're blessed by each other's sticky-handed children and disheveled laundry piles in the corner.

The crux of Advent is Emmanuel, God with us. Christ came to our messy earth, our busyness, our imperfection. We embody the heart of Advent when we mutually invite ourselves into one another's lives. Care about people worldwide, but not at the expense of the souls on your street.

Pray Psalm 37:3-7.

*Trust in the L*ORD*, and do good;*
so you will live in the land, and enjoy security.
*Take delight in the L*ORD*,*
and he will give you the desires of your heart.
*Commit your way to the L*ORD*;*
trust in him, and he will act.
He will make your vindication shine like the light,
and the justice of your cause like the noonday.
*Be still before the L*ORD*, and wait patiently for him;*
do not fret over those who prosper in their way,
over those who carry out evil devices.

The word of the Lord. Thanks be to God.

ASK:

In what ways can you bless those around you this week?

LISTEN:

"Hope" by John Arndt and David Gungor

REFLECT:

Christmas Scene (twentieth century) by Kim Heung Jong

FRIDAY

**Light the first purple or blue candle,
then the second purple or blue candle.**

Read:

There is no shortage of voices vying for our attention in our hyperconnected world. We are in far greater need for silence and stillness than we are for wisdom from other human beings who are so often eager to share their sage advice. These people may be well intentioned, but with our ability to hear from them instantaneously, at the click of a button, it's easy to rely on their finite prudence rather than the discernment that comes from our all-knowing, good God.

What would it look like to turn off a few loud voices this season? It might help you more clearly see life's moving shadow-patterns and hear the quiet voice of the Lord, leading your steps on the darkened path. God provides a flicker of candlelight just when we need it, but we might miss it if we're too focused on the din of voices vying for our precious attention.

Whose voices are you listening to this season? Are you able to hear God in the midst of the noise?

Pray Psalm 31:3-4,23-24.
You are indeed my rock and my fortress;
for your name's sake lead me and guide me,
take me out of the net that is hidden for me,
for you are my refuge...

*Love the L*ORD*, all you his saints.*
*The L*ORD *preserves the faithful,*
but abundantly repays the one who acts haughtily.
Be strong, and let your heart take courage,
*all you who wait for the L*ORD*.*
The word of the Lord. Thanks be to God.

ASK:

In what ways can you quiet the noise around you this week?

LISTEN:

"Let All Mortal Flesh Keep Silence" by Gerard Moultrie

REFLECT:

Guatemalan Nativity (1990s) by John Giuliani

SATURDAY

Light the first purple or blue candle,
then the second purple or blue candle.

Read:

Lighting the candle of faith acknowledges that faith is necessary for God to do good work in our lives. We often depend on faith, because it is hard to trust that there is unseen goodness and glory at work.

Our faith—our trust that God is good, real, and present—reminds us that Advent is worthy of remembering. It's an ongoing, inward practice of letting go, of choosing to believe even when we're not sure it makes sense. It reminds us that we're made to have faith, because otherwise our good God would have displayed all life's answers before us. Faith reminds us that we need a Savior and that because of him we're worthy of being saved.

As you move further into Advent, deeper into light and away from shadows, you may still be commemorating the season more as an act of faith than as an innate by-product of joy. If so, hold on to the reminder that faith begets faith and that when we cry out like the father of the sick child, "I believe; help my unbelief!" (Mark 9:24), Jesus is faithful to help us.

Pray Psalm 32:1-7.

Happy are those whose transgression is forgiven,

whose sin is covered.

Happy are those to whom the Lord imputes no iniquity,

and in whose spirit there is no deceit.

While I kept silence, my body wasted away

through my groaning all day long.

For day and night your hand was heavy upon me;

my strength was dried up as by the heat of summer. Selah

Then I acknowledged my sin to you,

and I did not hide my iniquity;

I said, "I will confess my transgressions to the LORD,"

and you forgave the guilt of my sin. Selah

Therefore let all who are faithful

offer prayer to you;

at a time of distress, the rush of mighty waters

shall not reach them.

You are a hiding place for me;

you preserve me from trouble;

you surround me with glad cries of deliverance. Selah

The word of the Lord. Thanks be to God.

ASK:

In what ways have you enjoyed the season of Advent this week?

LISTEN:

"Immanuel" by Jason Morant

REFLECT:

Be Not Afraid (2019) by Scott Erickson

ANTICIPATION

Anticipation lifts the heart. Desire is created to be fulfilled—
perhaps not all at once, more likely in slow stages... A softening of
hard-heartedness, a lively expectation, would herald the coming
of Messiah. And once again, in this season of Advent, the same
promise for the same Anointed One is coming closer.

LUCI SHAW[7]

SUNDAY

Light the first and second purple or blue candles,
then the pink candle.

Read:

This past week, we embodied our faith with preparation, both inward and outward. When we remember for what we have prepared, we can welcome joy into our lives, even when we don't feel quite ready, deserving, or willing. There is joy simply by entrusting our work to the God who loves us, cares for us, and wants us to rest in the work of Christ.

This is the third week of Advent, which means it's the second half of the season, and you're inching closer and closer to Christmas. Does this spark joyful anticipation in you? Or are you overshadowed by an inward panic as you think of all that you'd still like to accomplish before the season turns?

Remember that Advent is a gift, meant to be useful and enjoyable. God delights in *our* delight, and there is great delight in anticipating the feast to come. You can still focus on your to-do list, but make time today to sit and revel in the true joy that comes with this season of waiting on God, who has fulfilled the promise of redemption through the incarnate Christ.

Pray Psalm 63:1-8.

O God, you are my God, I seek you,
my soul thirsts for you;
my flesh faints for you,

66

as in a dry and weary land where there is no water.

So I have looked upon you in the sanctuary,

beholding your power and glory.

Because your steadfast love is better than life,

my lips will praise you.

So I will bless you as long as I live;

I will lift up my hands and call on your name.

My soul is satisfied as with a rich feast,

and my mouth praises you with joyful lips

when I think of you on my bed,

and meditate on you in the watches of the night;

for you have been my help,

and in the shadow of your wings I sing for joy.

My soul clings to you;

your right hand upholds me.

The word of the Lord. Thanks be to God.

ASK:

What is your honest hope for this third week of Advent?

LISTEN:

"Messiah" by Bifrost Arts

REFLECT:

Adoration of the Shepherds (1622) by Gerard van Honthorst

MONDAY

**Light the first and second purple or blue candles,
then the pink candle.**

Read:

Happiness is a lovely thing, especially during the holiday season, but it feels so fleeting to chase it. Happiness is wholly dependent on outside circumstances, on things beyond our control. The company holiday party went just as expected; the kids are content in their reasonable Christmas expectations; the cookies turned out delicious; the ordered gifts weren't overpriced; the extended family member was gracious in their latest phone call.

But joy is wholly dependent on one's inward posture, on remembering God's never-changing love for us. *Feeling* joyful isn't required for acknowledging that there is real, genuine joy found in the incarnate Christ. Life may be difficult at the moment, in this holiday season. It might not be happy. But it can be joy filled when we remember, by faith, that God is Emmanuel—he is with us.

Lean into the inward joy of knowing, even if there's no accompanying joyful spirit. The incarnate Christ is here with you as you anticipate the celebration of his birth.

Pray Psalm 41:1-3.
*Happy are those who consider the poor;
the Lord delivers them in the day of trouble.*

The LʚRD protects them and keeps them alive;
they are called happy in the land.
You do not give them up to the will of their enemies.
The LʚRD sustains them on their sickbed;
in their illness you heal all their infirmities.
The word of the Lord. Thanks be to God.

ASK:

What brings you joy right now?

LISTEN:

"All Shall Be Well" by Ben Keyes, Peter La Grand, and Jill McFadden

REFLECT:

The Birth of Christ (1896) by Paul Gauguin

TUESDAY

Light the first and second purple or blue candles,
then the pink candle.

Read:

There is a story from Czech bishop Monsignor Hnilica of a Christmas Eve with Saint Teresa of Calcutta. There was a knock on the convent's door during their simple but festive dinner, and the nun who went to answer the door returned with a basket covered in a cloth. "A woman gave it to me, then rushed off," she said—then added as she handed the basket to Teresa, "She was probably a benefactor who wanted to donate some food to us for Christmas."

Teresa's eyes sparkled as she removed the cloth and lifted up a sleeping baby boy. "Jesus has arrived," she said with a smile. The baby was only a few days old, and the boy's mother had probably entrusted him to the nuns because she felt unable to raise him.

The boy woke up and began to cry. Teresa said with tears in her eyes, "Look, now we can say that our Christmas is complete. Baby Jesus has come to us."[8]

God's Son was delivered to us by taking on human flesh as a baby boy, and God continues to come to us and remind us of Christ's Incarnation. Look for ways, large or small, in your world this week that God may be coming to your doorstep, arriving in the most unexpected forms.

Pray Psalm 47:1-7.
Clap your hands, all you peoples;

shout to God with loud songs of joy.

*For the L*ORD*, the Most High, is awesome,*

a great king over all the earth.

He subdued peoples under us,

and nations under our feet.

He chose our heritage for us,

the pride of Jacob whom he loves. Selah

God has gone up with a shout,

*the L*ORD *with the sound of a trumpet.*

Sing praises to God, sing praises;

sing praises to our King, sing praises.

For God is the king of all the earth;

sing praises with a psalm.

The word of the Lord. Thanks be to God.

ASK:

In what ways could you meet a need around you this week?

LISTEN:

"Wonder (Advent)" by Pedro de la Cruz and Colleen Nixon

REFLECT:

God Is with Us (2006) by Hanna Varghese

WEEK 3

WEDNESDAY

Light the first and second purple or blue candles,
then the pink candle.

Read:

In recognizing the season of Advent, we look for the coming of the one who has already delivered us from evil, who will continue to deliver us from evil, and who will one day deliver the final blow to all earthly evil. Deliverance happens all the time, in small ways and large, when we choose to resist evil wherever it appears.

The idea of evil might be cosmic on a grand scale, but for most of us, it appears in subtle disguises: rejection, sorrow, suffering, poverty, hunger. Our neighbor's lack, real or perceived, can drive a wedge between them and their maker, who wants their life to be full and alive.

We can join in God's deliverance when we resist these small evils. We remember the incarnate Christ, who came to earth to deliver us from all evil, when we share our listening ear, wipe tears from wet eyes, watch our neighbors' children so moms can work, and bring a casserole to a lonely friend.

Advent is the dawn of the cosmic battle over which there is already victory, and we remember Christ's victory again and again by bearing one another's burdens.

Pray Psalm 119:65-68.

You have dealt well with your servant,
O Lord, according to your word.
Teach me good judgment and knowledge,

for I believe in your commandments.
Before I was humbled I went astray,
but now I keep your word.
You are good and do good;
teach me your statutes.
The word of the Lord. Thanks be to God.

ASK:

Where can you see God's deliverance, even in the midst of sorrow?

LISTEN:

"Kyrie 2007" by Bruce Benedict

REFLECT:

The Nativity (1891) by Gari Melchers

THURSDAY

Light the first and second purple or blue candles,
then the pink candle.

Read:

We would be remiss if, in this week of Advent when we remember joy, we did not stop to remember the beauty surrounding us: the spice of gingerbread wafting through the air, the earnest paper snowflakes taped haphazardly to the windows, or perhaps the joy of choosing to give fewer presents in exchange for giving more time to others who need our undivided attention.

Regardless of what's scribbled on the squares of your calendar this week, take time to intentionally pause and notice beauty. Notice the charm of a child's disjointed retelling of a story with a twinkle in her eye, the snap of twigs in the cold air, and the crunch of leaves underneath your feet on your morning walk. Remember the fullness of God's love for us, how the world's beauty is a gift for us to steward and be captivated by. We can savor these sunset days of Advent while the candlelight dances with joy in the hope of God's coming.

Pray Psalm 33:4-8.
*The word of the L*ORD *is upright,*
and all his work is done in faithfulness.
He loves righteousness and justice;
*the earth is full of the steadfast love of the L*ORD.

By the word of the Lord the heavens were made,
and all their host by the breath of his mouth.
He gathered the waters of the sea as in a bottle;
he put the deeps in storehouses.
Let all the earth fear the Lord;
let all the inhabitants of the world stand in awe of him.
The word of the Lord. Thanks be to God.

ASK:

Where did you see God's beauty today?

LISTEN:

"Creator of the Stars of Night"

REFLECT:

The Starry Night (1889) by Vincent van Gogh

FRIDAY

Light the first and second purple or blue candles,
then the pink candle.

Read:

While we long for a complete fullness of joy this Advent season, we are given the gift of free joy right now. In the hustle of the later days leading to Christmastide, as the world rushes to make Christmas Day perfect, we can rest in quiet assurance that all will be well.

As you look forward to the full dawning of Christmas light, growing brighter and brighter as the Advent days come closer to an end, rest in the joy found in quiet moments, either in solitude or surrounded by others in celebration. Listen to God's voice; let it wash over you with love as you anticipate the full joy of Christ's arrival. God's grace is what gives us the faith and hope to wait with eager anticipation.

Pray Psalm 40:1-3.

I waited patiently for the Lord;
he inclined to me and heard my cry.
He drew me up from the desolate pit,
out of the miry bog,
and set my feet upon a rock,
making my steps secure.
He put a new song in my mouth,

a song of praise to our God.

Many will see and fear,

*and put their trust in the L*ORD.

The word of the Lord. Thanks be to God.

ASK:

In what ways can you slow down right now, even in a busy season?

LISTEN:

"Show Us the King" by John Arndt and David Gungor

REFLECT:

Unto Us a Child Is Born (1998) by Hanna Varghese

SATURDAY

Light the first and second purple or blue candles,
then the pink candle.

Read:

Take joy in knowing that, even if the Advent season isn't always full of cheer or glad anticipation, Jesus knows your longing for joy in the midst of it. There are days when snow falls gently outside the front window and a roast is in the oven; there are also days when muddy-gray slush fills our tire treads and dinner is haphazard and piecemeal. There are seasons when there is enough and seasons when we have to do without.

Dorothy Sayers once remarked, "[God] has Himself gone through the whole of human experience, from the trivial irritations of family life and the cramping restrictions of hard work and lack of money to the worst horrors of pain and humiliation, defeat, despair, and death. When He was a man, He played the man. He was born in poverty and died in disgrace and thought it well worthwhile."[9]

Christ finds it worthwhile to come incarnate, in full humanity, and to know the fullness of our joys and sorrows. God meets you here in Advent, in the shadows, and brings the light of knowing well your full experience of life on earth. Jesus is truly Emmanuel, God with us. In this we find true joy.

Pray Psalm 138:4-8.

All the kings of the earth shall praise you, O Lord,
for they have heard the words of your mouth.

They shall sing of the ways of the L<small>ORD</small>,

for great is the glory of the L<small>ORD</small>.

For though the L<small>ORD</small> is high, he regards the lowly;

but the haughty he perceives from far away.

Though I walk in the midst of trouble,

you preserve me against the wrath of my enemies;

you stretch out your hand,

and your right hand delivers me.

The L<small>ORD</small> will fulfill his purpose for me;

your steadfast love, O L<small>ORD</small>, endures forever.

Do not forsake the work of your hands.

The word of the Lord. Thanks be to God.

ASK:

In what ways have you enjoyed the season of Advent this week?

LISTEN:

"Comfort, Comfort Now My People" by Latifah Phillips and David Wilton
(original hymn by Johann Olearius)

REFLECT:

The Christ Window (1970) at Fraumünster Church in Zurich, by Marc Chagall

GRATITUDE

Blessed is the season which engages the whole world in a conspiracy of love!

HAMILTON WRIGHT MABIE[10]

SUNDAY (or December 18)

Light the first and second purple or blue candles, the pink candle, and then the remaining purple or blue candle. *(Note: Only light the fourth candle if it's the fourth week of Advent.)*

Read John 3:16-21.

God so loved the world that he gave his only Son, so that everyone who believes in him may not perish but may have eternal life. Indeed, God did not send the Son into the world to condemn the world, but in order that the world might be saved through him. Those who believe in him are not condemned; but those who do not believe are condemned already, because they have not believed in the name of the only Son of God. And this is the judgment, that the light has come into the world, and people loved darkness rather than light because their deeds were evil. For all who do evil hate the light and do not come to the light, so that their deeds may not be exposed. But those who do what is true come to the light, so that it may be clearly seen that their deeds have been done in God.

The word of the Lord. Thanks be to God.

Read:

The light is growing brighter in these final days of Advent. We look ahead to the arrival of Emmanuel, God with us, who comes that the world might be renewed and victorious over evil's darkness.

Living in a post-birth-of-Christ world, we forget what it must have been like to wait in darkness, wondering if God had forgotten the Jewish people oppressed under Roman rule. There was no sign that God was in a hurry to fulfill the promise made centuries before, the promise that one day there would be one who would rescue them from the shadows of evil. They waited, and waited, and waited, with no sign that God remembered them.

Christ is the reminder that God remembers us. He came to the world not only to save it, but to drown out the evils of the earth with the light of salvation. With seven days until the dawn of Christmas, we wait.

ASK:

What is your honest hope for this last week of Advent?

LISTEN:

"For the Beauty of the Earth" by Folliott Pierpoint

REFLECT:

The Birth of Jesus Christ (1952–1953) by Woonbo Kim Ki-chang

MONDAY (or December 19)

Light the first and second purple or blue candles, the pink candle, and then the remaining purple or blue candle. *(Note: Only light the fourth candle if it's the fourth week of Advent.)*

Read Luke 1:5-7,10-20,24-25.

In the days of King Herod of Judea, there was a priest named Zechariah, who belonged to the priestly order of Abijah. His wife was a descendant of Aaron, and her name was Elizabeth. Both of them were righteous before God, living blamelessly according to all the commandments and regulations of the Lord. But they had no children, because Elizabeth was barren, and both were getting on in years...

Now at the time of the incense offering, the whole assembly of the people was praying outside. Then there appeared to him an angel of the Lord, standing at the right side of the altar of incense. When Zechariah saw him, he was terrified; and fear overwhelmed him. But the angel said to him, "Do not be afraid, Zechariah, for your prayer has been heard. Your wife Elizabeth will bear you a son, and you will name him John. You will have joy and gladness, and many will rejoice at his birth, for he will be great in the sight of the Lord. He must never drink wine or strong drink; even before his birth he will be filled with the Holy Spirit. He will turn many of the people of Israel to the Lord their God. With the spirit and power of Elijah he will go before him, to turn the hearts of parents to their children, and the disobedient to the wisdom of the righteous, to make ready a people prepared for the Lord." Zechariah said to the angel, "How will I know that this is so? For I am an old man, and my wife is getting on in years." The angel replied, "I am Gabriel. I stand in the presence of God, and I have been sent to speak to you and to bring you this good news. But now, because you did not believe my words, which will be fulfilled in their time, you will become mute, unable to speak, until the day these things occur…

After those days his wife Elizabeth conceived, and for five months she remained in seclusion. She said, "This is what the Lord has done for me when he looked favorably on me and took away the disgrace I have endured among my people."

The word of the Lord. Thanks be to God.

Read:

John the Baptist was a lantern, leading people toward the bonfire of the incarnate Christ. Elizabeth's model of glad trust, Zechariah's example of eventual belief (see Luke 1:59-64), and John's humble life of simplicity and service are reminders to us in these last few days of Advent that God has come for all and to all, regardless of our posture. Whether we *feel* trust in God, Christ comes among us, to love us and live with us.

ASK:
Where did you see the light of God today?

LISTEN:
"Zechariah's Song" by Ben Keyes, Peter La Grand, and Jill McFadden

REFLECT:
The Annunciation of the Angel to Zacharias (1486–1490) by Domenico Ghirlandaio

TUESDAY (or December 20)

Light the first and second purple or blue candles, the pink candle, and then the remaining purple or blue candle. *(Note: Only light the fourth candle if it's the fourth week of Advent.)*

Read Luke 1:26-38.

In the sixth month the angel Gabriel was sent by God to a town in Galilee called Nazareth, to a virgin engaged to a man whose name was Joseph, of the house of David. The virgin's name was Mary. And he came to her and said, "Greetings, favored one! The Lord is with you." But she was much perplexed by his words and pondered what sort of greeting this might be. The angel said to her, "Do not be afraid, Mary, for you have found favor with God. And now, you will conceive in your womb and bear a son, and you will name him Jesus. He will be great, and will be called the Son of the Most High, and the Lord God will give to him the throne of his ancestor David. He will reign over the house of Jacob forever, and of his kingdom there will be no end." Mary said to the angel, "How can this be, since I am a virgin?" The angel said to her, "The Holy Spirit will come upon you, and the power of the Most High will overshadow you; therefore the child to be born will be holy; he will be called Son of God. And now, your relative Elizabeth in her old age has also conceived a son; and this is the sixth month for her who was said to be barren. For nothing will be impossible with God." Then Mary said, "Here am I, the servant of the Lord; let it be with me according to your word." Then the angel departed from her.

The word of the Lord. Thanks be to God.

Read:

God saw fit to tuck the Savior of the world into an unremarkable town through an unassuming Jewish girl. Christ—who Scripture says was there in the beginning of everything and through whom all things came into being—willingly chose to set aside his omniscience and omnipresence in exchange for finite human knowledge and the limitation of a few square miles in the Middle East. Christ became Emmanuel out of love for us. The one of whom Scripture says, "Without him not one thing came into being" (John 1:3), chose to embody the most helpless form of humankind and come right into poverty and oppression. What deep, extravagant, incomprehensible love!

ASK:

Where did you see the light of God today?

LISTEN:

"Gabriel's Message" (original source unknown)

REFLECT:

The Annunciation (2000) by John Collier

WEDNESDAY (or December 21)

Light the first and second purple or blue candles, the pink candle, and then the remaining purple or blue candle. *(Note: Only light the fourth candle if it's the fourth week of Advent.)*

Read Luke 1:41-42,45-55.

Elizabeth was filled with the Holy Spirit and exclaimed with a loud cry, "Blessed are you among women, and blessed is the fruit of your womb... And blessed is she who believed that there would be a fulfillment of what was spoken to her by the Lord."

And Mary said,

"My soul magnifies the Lord,

and my spirit rejoices in God my Savior,

for he has looked with favor on the lowliness of his servant.

Surely, from now on all generations will call me blessed;

for the Mighty One has done great things for me,

and holy is his name.

His mercy is for those who fear him

from generation to generation.

He has shown strength with his arm;

he has scattered the proud in the thoughts of their hearts.

He has brought down the powerful from their thrones,

and lifted up the lowly;

he has filled the hungry with good things,

and sent the rich away empty.

He has helped his servant Israel,

in remembrance of his mercy,

according to the promise he made to our ancestors,

to Abraham and to his descendants forever."

The word of the Lord. Thanks be to God.

Read:

Because we know Mary treasured God's word and pondered it in her heart, we can assume she knew well the Old Testament words of Hannah, Samuel's mother (1 Samuel 2:1-10). Her Magnificat here mimics Hannah's praise to God. Perhaps Mary prayed or sang these words many times, etching them into the rhythms of her life. "The Mighty One has done great things for me, and holy is his name" (Luke 1:49) might have been a natural outpouring and response to the movement of God in her life already.

From her responses to Gabriel and Elizabeth and onward throughout her pregnancy and into motherhood, Mary embodied a sacrificial life of trust in God. May Mary's posture of praise for God's plan be our example as we near the end of Advent. May we trust in God's faithfulness, shown time and again for thousands of years.

ASK:

Where did you see the light of God today?

LISTEN:

"Mother of God" by John Arndt and David Gungor

REFLECT:

Mary and Eve (2003) by Grace Remington

THURSDAY (or December 22)

Light the first and second purple or blue candles, the pink candle, and then the remaining purple or blue candle. *(Note: Only light the fourth candle if it's the fourth week of Advent.)*

Read Luke 1:67-79.

His father Zechariah was filled with the Holy Spirit and spoke this prophecy:
"Blessed be the Lord God of Israel,
for he has looked favorably on his people and redeemed them.
He has raised up a mighty savior for us
in the house of his servant David,
as he spoke through the mouth of his holy prophets from of old, that we
would be saved from our enemies and from the hand of all who hate us.
Thus he has shown the mercy promised to our ancestors,
and has remembered his holy covenant,
the oath that he swore to our ancestor Abraham,
to grant us that we, being rescued from the hands of our enemies,
might serve him without fear, in holiness and righteousness
before him all our days.
And you, child, will be called the prophet of the Most High;
for you will go before the Lord to prepare his ways,
to give knowledge of salvation to his people
by the forgiveness of their sins.

By the tender mercy of our God,
the dawn from on high will break upon us,
to give light to those who sit in darkness and in the shadow of death,
to guide our feet into the way of peace."
The word of the Lord. Thanks be to God.

Read:

After John the Baptist is born, his father, Zechariah, regains his speech and shares this prophecy given by the Holy Spirit. He looks back, remembering God's favor over faithful generations, and then looks forward, naming his son's role in preparing people for salvation through Christ. Zechariah remembers God's faithfulness in the past and puts his hope in God's faithfulness for the future.

With only a few days remaining in the season of Advent, the light of Christ burns brighter. May we remember how God has led us over the past few weeks and place our trust in him through the coming days of Christmastide. God brings light to guide our feet in the way of peace.

ASK:

Where did you see the light of God today?

LISTEN:

"Praise God from Whom All Blessings Flow" by Thomas Ken

REFLECT:

Nativity (2002) by Sawai Chinnawong

FRIDAY (or December 23)

Light the first and second purple or blue candles, the pink candle, and then the remaining purple or blue candle. *(Note: Only light the fourth candle if it's the fourth week of Advent.)*

Read Isaiah 11:1-2,6-9.

A shoot shall come out from the stump of Jesse,

and a branch shall grow out of his roots.

The spirit of the Lord shall rest on him,

the spirit of wisdom and understanding,

the spirit of counsel and might,

the spirit of knowledge and the fear of the Lord...

The wolf shall live with the lamb,

the leopard shall lie down with the kid,

the calf and the lion and the fatling together,

and a little child shall lead them.

The cow and the bear shall graze,

their young shall lie down together;

and the lion shall eat straw like the ox.

The nursing child shall play over the hole of the asp,

and the weaned child shall put its hand on the adder's den.

They will not hurt or destroy

on all my holy mountain;

for the earth will be full of the knowledge of the Lord

as the waters cover the sea.
The word of the Lord. Thanks be to God.

Read:

More than 700 years before Jesus was born in Bethlehem, the prophet Isaiah depicted Christ's arrival with the world turning on its head. Someone filled with wisdom, understanding, counsel, and might would advocate for the poor and meek of the earth, the ones oppressed by the wicked. Predators would live in harmony with prey, animal instincts would quiet, and even vulnerable young children could play without fear of a dangerous world. Creation would reorder itself.

But 2,000 years beyond Jesus's time on earth, we know this isn't how life in our fallen world works. Children are still in danger, lions are still carnivores, and wolves still hunt sheep. Isaiah's prophecy is not yet fully complete, so this poetry describes hope for our future, hope for the light still to come.

This is the already-but-not-yet paradox we live with in our Advent season: that Christ has come, and that Christ will still come. Light is growing brighter as we come closer to Christmas Day, but there will be one day when the light will right all wrongs and the whole earth will embody peace. This is what we wait for with grateful expectation when we wait for Christmas.

ASK:
Where did you see the light of God today?

LISTEN:
"Heaven Meets Earth" by Leslie Jordan and David Leonard

REFLECT:
Nativity (2006) by Brian Kershisnik

93

CHRISTMAS EVE

Light the first and second purple or blue candles, the pink candle,
and then the remaining purple or blue candle.

Read Luke 2:7-20.

[Mary] gave birth to her firstborn son and wrapped him in bands of cloth, and laid him in a manger, because there was no place for them in the inn.

In that region there were shepherds living in the fields, keeping watch over their flock by night. Then an angel of the Lord stood before them, and the glory of the Lord shone around them, and they were terrified. But the angel said to them, "Do not be afraid; for see—I am bringing you good news of great joy for all the people: to you is born this day in the city of David a Savior, who is the Messiah, the Lord. This will be a sign for you: you will find a child wrapped in bands of cloth and lying in a manger." And suddenly there was with the angel a multitude of the heavenly host, praising God and saying,

"Glory to God in the highest heaven,

and on earth peace among those whom he favors!"

When the angels had left them and gone into heaven, the shepherds said to one another, "Let us go now to Bethlehem and see this thing that has taken place, which the Lord has made known to us." So they went with haste and found Mary and Joseph, and the child lying in the manger. When they saw this, they made known what had been told them about this child; and all who heard it were amazed at what the shepherds told them. But Mary treasured all these words and pondered them in her heart. The shepherds returned, glorify-

ing and praising God for all they had heard and seen, as it had been told them.
The word of the Lord. Thanks be to God.

Read:

If the primary goal in the birth of the Messiah was worldwide fanfare, breaking news, or shout-from-the-rooftop celebration, God sure chose a strange way to orchestrate all its events. Based on the evidence, it seems safe to reason there was quite a different sort of fanfare in mind. From the very beginning of time, starting with Eve's redemption through a teenage peasant girl to Gabriel first announcing Christ's birth not to kings and emperors but to the lowliest of the low, God has flipped the script on the expected.

It makes no sense to welcome he who would right all earthly wrongs and swing wide the heavenly gates during the oppressive Roman Empire, under the thumbs of Augustus and Herod, through the Jewish people seen as inconvenient foreigners at best. In Jesus's birth, God chooses to do the unthinkable: save the whole world by first making the most unimpressive of entrances.

The shepherds are rightly terrified at this news, coming from an alien being telling them to not be afraid. Yet of course God would choose to first celebrate the Son of Man with grubby peasants tucked in the valleys of hills. This has always been the way, from the garden to now: the last shall be first, grace covers fully the vilest of vile, God's ways are not our ways. As of now, the moment of his birth and onward, Jesus will continue to surprise and astonish us.

May we all be like Mary entering this Christmas season: pondering the wonders of God in our hearts, our faces aimed toward the treasured light, beaming like the sun through broken shadows. At this moment, the world is on its way to full redemption, where the shepherds, Magi, animals, and Joseph and Mary wait expectantly in the world's already-not-yet state of full anticipation. This holiday season, we continue to wait with them still, sitting in the shadows of the earth where light has cracked through.

Christmas Day

Light the first and second purple or blue candles, the pink candle, the remaining purple or blue candle, and then the white candle.

Read 1 John 4:9-15.

God's love was revealed among us in this way: God sent his only Son into the world so that we might live through him. In this is love, not that we loved God but that he loved us and sent his Son to be the atoning sacrifice for our sins. Beloved, since God loved us so much, we also ought to love one another. No one has ever seen God; if we love one another, God lives in us, and his love is perfected in us.

By this we know that we abide in him and he in us, because he has given us of his Spirit. And we have seen and do testify that the Father has sent his Son as the Savior of the world. God abides in those who confess that Jesus is the Son of God, and they abide in God.

The word of the Lord. Thanks be to God.

Read:

We have walked the journey of Advent, from shadow into light, and now it is the dawn of Christmastide. We celebrate that Christ is Emmanuel, God with us! He was born for all humankind, as Savior to all.

In our already-but-not-yet world in which we live, what do we do now? What do we do with the knowledge that Jesus has already been born, died, and was resurrected for the redemption of the world—and yet we still wait in hope for the true fullness of redemption, when all wrongs will be made right?

We love each other. We reveal God's love each day when we love one another.

This is how we abide in Christ: We let the love of God, first fully shown to us through the miracle of Jesus's arrival celebrated on Christmas Day, pour out of us and onto others. This is how we live in the shadows while celebrating the glorious light of Christ's birth.

Daily love, daily confession of Christ as Messiah for the world. The light we long for during Advent is already in us, because God abides in us. Let the hope, faith, joy, and peace of Christmastide abide in you, starting today, as you celebrate the arrival of Christ. He is born—alleluia!

ASK:

Where do you hope to see God today?

LISTEN:

Messiah by George Frideric Handel (I recommend the song "Handel's Messiah" performed by Jenny and Tyler.)

REFLECT:

Adoration of the Shepherds (1644) by Georges de La Tour

ADDITIONS

Into this world, this demented inn, in which there is
absolutely no room for Him at all, Christ has come uninvited.

THOMAS MERTON[11]

ALTERNATIVE SCRIPTURE READINGS

DECEMBER 1

John 1:1-18 NLT

In the beginning the Word already existed. The Word was with God, and the Word was God. He existed in the beginning with God. God created everything through him, and nothing was created except through him. The Word gave life to everything that was created, and his life brought light to everyone. The light shines in the darkness, and the darkness can never extinguish it.

God sent a man, John the Baptist, to tell about the light so that everyone might believe because of his testimony. John himself was not the light; he was simply a witness to tell about the light. The one who is the true light, who gives light to everyone, was coming into the world.

He came into the very world he created, but the world didn't recognize him. He came to his own people, and even they rejected him. But to all who believed him and accepted him, he gave the right to become children of God. They are reborn—not with a physical birth resulting from human passion or plan, but a birth that comes from God.

So the Word became human and made his home among us. He was full of unfailing love and faithfulness. And we have seen his glory, the glory of the Father's one and only Son. John testified about him when he shouted to the crowds, "This is the one I was talking about when I said, 'Someone is coming after me who is far greater than I am, for he existed long before me.'"

From his abundance we have all received one gracious blessing after another. For the law was given through Moses, but God's unfailing love and faithfulness came through Jesus Christ. No one has ever seen God. But the unique One, who is himself God, is near to the Father's heart. He has revealed God to us.

When Herod was king of Judea, there was a Jewish priest named Zechariah. He was a member of the priestly order of Abijah, and his wife, Elizabeth, was also from the priestly line of Aaron. Zechariah and Elizabeth were righteous in God's eyes, careful to obey all of the Lord's commandments and regulations. They had no children because Elizabeth was unable to conceive, and they were both very old.

One day Zechariah was serving God in the Temple, for his order was on duty that week. As was the custom of the priests, he was chosen by lot to enter the sanctuary of the Lord and burn incense. While the incense was being burned, a great crowd stood outside, praying.

While Zechariah was in the sanctuary, an angel of the Lord appeared to him, standing to the right of the incense altar. Zechariah was shaken and overwhelmed with fear when he saw him. But the angel said, "Don't be afraid, Zechariah! God has heard your prayer. Your wife, Elizabeth, will give you a son, and you are to name him John. You will have great joy and gladness, and many will rejoice at his birth, for he will be great in the eyes of the Lord. He must never touch wine or other alcoholic drinks. He will be filled with the Holy Spirit, even before his birth. And he will turn many Israelites to the Lord their God. He will be a man with the spirit and power of Elijah. He will prepare the people for the coming of the Lord. He will turn the hearts of the fathers to their children, and he will cause those who are rebellious to accept the wisdom of the godly."

Zechariah said to the angel, "How can I be sure this will happen? I'm an old man now, and my wife is also well along in years."

Then the angel said, "I am Gabriel! I stand in the very presence of God. It was he who sent me to bring you this good news! But now, since you didn't believe what I said, you will be silent and unable to speak until the child is born. For my words will certainly be fulfilled at the proper time."

Meanwhile, the people were waiting for Zechariah to come out of the sanctuary, wondering why he was taking so long. When he finally did come out, he couldn't speak to them. Then they realized from his gestures and his silence that he must have seen a vision in the sanctuary.

When Zechariah's week of service in the Temple was over, he returned home. Soon afterward his wife, Elizabeth, became pregnant and went into seclusion for five months. "How kind the Lord is!" she exclaimed. "He has taken away my disgrace of having no children."

In the sixth month of Elizabeth's pregnancy, God sent the angel Gabriel to Nazareth, a village in Galilee, to a virgin named Mary. She was engaged to be married to a man named Joseph, a descendant of King David. Gabriel appeared to her and said, "Greetings, favored woman! The Lord is with you!"

Confused and disturbed, Mary tried to think what the angel could mean. "Don't be afraid, Mary," the angel told her, "for you have found favor with God! You will conceive and give birth to a son, and you will name him Jesus. He will be very great and will be called the Son of the Most High. The Lord God will give him the throne of his ancestor David. And he will reign over Israel forever; his Kingdom will never end!"

Mary asked the angel, "But how can this happen? I am a virgin."

The angel replied, "The Holy Spirit will come upon you, and the power of the Most High will overshadow you. So the baby to be born will be holy, and he will be called the Son of God. What's more, your relative Elizabeth has become pregnant in her old age! People used to say she was barren, but she has conceived a son and is now in her sixth month. For the word of God will never fail."

Mary responded, "I am the Lord's servant. May everything you have said about me come true." And then the angel left her.

A few days later Mary hurried to the hill country of Judea, to the town where Zechariah lived. She entered the house and greeted Elizabeth. At the sound of Mary's greeting, Elizabeth's child leaped within her, and Elizabeth was filled with the Holy Spirit.

Elizabeth gave a glad cry and exclaimed to Mary, "God has blessed you above all women, and your child is blessed. Why am I so honored, that the mother of my Lord should visit me? When I heard your greeting, the baby in my womb jumped for joy. You are blessed because you believed that the Lord would do what he said."

Mary responded,

"Oh, how my soul praises the Lord.

How my spirit rejoices in God my Savior!

For he took notice of his lowly servant girl,

and from now on all generations will call me blessed.

For the Mighty One is holy,

and he has done great things for me.

He shows mercy from generation to generation

to all who fear him.

His mighty arm has done tremendous things!

He has scattered the proud and haughty ones.

He has brought down princes from their thrones

and exalted the humble.

He has filled the hungry with good things

and sent the rich away with empty hands.

He has helped his servant Israel

and remembered to be merciful.

For he made this promise to our ancestors,

to Abraham and his children forever."

Mary stayed with Elizabeth about three months and then went back to her own home.

When it was time for Elizabeth's baby to be born, she gave birth to a son. And when her neighbors and relatives heard that the Lord had been very merciful to her, everyone rejoiced with her.

When the baby was eight days old, they all came for the circumcision ceremony. They wanted to name him Zechariah, after his father. But Elizabeth said, "No! His name is John!"

"What?" they exclaimed. "There is no one in all your family by that name." So they used gestures to ask the baby's father what he wanted to name him. He motioned for a writing tablet, and to everyone's surprise he wrote, "His name is John." Instantly Zechariah could speak again, and he began praising God.

Awe fell upon the whole neighborhood, and the news of what had happened spread throughout the Judean hills. Everyone who heard about it reflected on these events and asked, "What will this child turn out to be?" For the hand of the Lord was surely upon him in a special way.

Then his father, Zechariah, was filled with the Holy Spirit and gave this prophecy:

"Praise the Lord, the God of Israel,

because he has visited and redeemed his people.

He has sent us a mighty Savior

from the royal line of his servant David,

just as he promised

through his holy prophets long ago.

Now we will be saved from our enemies

and from all who hate us.

He has been merciful to our ancestors
>by remembering his sacred covenant—

the covenant he swore with an oath
>to our ancestor Abraham.

We have been rescued from our enemies
>so we can serve God without fear,

in holiness and righteousness
>for as long as we live.

"And you, my little son,
>will be called the prophet of the Most High,

>because you will prepare the way for the Lord.

You will tell his people how to find salvation
>through forgiveness of their sins.

Because of God's tender mercy,
>the morning light from heaven

>is about to break upon us,

to give light to those who sit in darkness and in the shadow of death,
>and to guide us to the path of peace."

John grew up and became strong in spirit. And he lived in the wilderness until he began his public ministry to Israel.

This is the Good News about Jesus the Messiah, the Son of God. It began just as the prophet Isaiah had written:

> "Look, I am sending my messenger ahead of you,
>> and he will prepare your way.
> He is a voice shouting in the wilderness,
> 'Prepare the way for the Lord's coming!
>> Clear the road for him!'"

This messenger was John the Baptist. He was in the wilderness and preached that people should be baptized to show that they had repented of their sins and turned to God to be forgiven. All of Judea, including all the people of Jerusalem, went out to see and hear John. And when they confessed their sins, he baptized them in the Jordan River. His clothes were woven from coarse camel hair, and he wore a leather belt around his waist. For food he ate locusts and wild honey.

John announced: "Someone is coming soon who is greater than I am—so much greater that I'm not even worthy to stoop down like a slave and untie the straps of his sandals. I baptize you with water, but he will baptize you with the Holy Spirit!"

This is how Jesus the Messiah was born. His mother, Mary, was engaged to be married to Joseph. But before the marriage took place, while she was still a virgin, she became pregnant through the power of the Holy Spirit. Joseph, to whom she was engaged, was a righteous man and did not want to disgrace her publicly, so he decided to break the engagement quietly.

As he considered this, an angel of the Lord appeared to him in a dream. "Joseph, son of David," the angel said, "do not be afraid to take Mary as your wife. For the child within her was conceived by the Holy Spirit. And she will have a son, and you are to name him Jesus, for he will save his people from their sins."

All of this occurred to fulfill the Lord's message through his prophet:

"Look! The virgin will conceive a child!
She will give birth to a son,
and they will call him Immanuel,
which means 'God is with us.'"

When Joseph woke up, he did as the angel of the Lord commanded and took Mary as his wife. But he did not have sexual relations with her until her son was born. And Joseph named him Jesus.

Jesus was about thirty years old when he began his public ministry.

Jesus was known as the son of Joseph. Joseph was the son of Heli. Heli was the son of Matthat. Matthat was the son of Levi. Levi was the son of Melki. Melki was the son of Jannai. Jannai was the son of Joseph. Joseph was the son of Mattathias. Mattathias was the son of Amos. Amos was the son of Nahum. Nahum was the son of Esli. Esli was the son of Naggai. Naggai was the son of Maath. Maath was the son of Mattathias. Mattathias was the son of Semein. Semein was the son of Josech. Josech was the son of Joda. Joda was the son of Joanan. Joanan was the son of Rhesa. Rhesa was the son of Zerubbabel. Zerubbabel was the son of Shealtiel. Shealtiel was the son of Neri. Neri was the son of Melki. Melki was the son of Addi. Addi was the son of Cosam. Cosam was the son of Elmadam. Elmadam was the son of Er. Er was the son of Joshua. Joshua was the son of Eliezer. Eliezer was the son of Jorim. Jorim was the son of Matthat. Matthat was the son of Levi. Levi was the son of Simeon. Simeon was the son of Judah. Judah was the son of Joseph. Joseph was the son of Jonam. Jonam was the son of Eliakim. Eliakim was the son of Melea. Melea was the son of Menna. Menna was the son of Mattatha. Mattatha was the son of Nathan. Nathan was the son of David. David was the son of Jesse. Jesse was the son of Obed. Obed was the son of Boaz. Boaz was the son of Salmon. Salmon was the son of Nahshon. Nahshon was the son of Amminadab. Amminadab was the son of Admin. Admin was the son of Arni. Arni was the son of Hezron. Hezron was the son of Perez. Perez was the son of Judah. Judah was the son of Jacob. Jacob was the son of Isaac. Isaac was the son of Abraham. Abraham was the son of Terah. Terah was the son of Nahor. Nahor was the son of Serug. Serug was the son of Reu. Reu was the son of Peleg. Peleg was the son of Eber. Eber was the son of Shelah. Shelah was the son of Cainan. Cainan was the son of Arphaxad. Arphaxad was the son of Shem. Shem was the son of Noah. Noah was the son of Lamech. Lamech was the son of Methuselah. Methuselah was the son of Enoch. Enoch was the son of Jared. Jared was the son of Mahalalel. Mahalalel was the son of Kenan. Kenan was the son of Enosh. Enosh was the son of Seth. Seth was the son of Adam. Adam was the son of God.

At that time the Roman emperor, Augustus, decreed that a census should be taken throughout the Roman Empire. (This was the first census taken when Quirinius was governor of Syria.) All returned to their own ancestral towns to register for this census. And because Joseph was a descendant of King David, he had to go to Bethlehem in Judea, David's ancient home. He traveled there from the village of Nazareth in Galilee. He took with him Mary, to whom he was engaged, who was now expecting a child.

And while they were there, the time came for her baby to be born. She gave birth to her firstborn son. She wrapped him snugly in strips of cloth and laid him in a manger, because there was no lodging available for them.

That night there were shepherds staying in the fields nearby, guarding their flocks of sheep. Suddenly, an angel of the Lord appeared among them, and the radiance of the Lord's glory surrounded them. They were terrified, but the angel reassured them. "Don't be afraid!" he said. "I bring you good news that will bring great joy to all people. The Savior—yes, the Messiah, the Lord—has been born today in Bethlehem, the city of David! And you will recognize him by this sign: You will find a baby wrapped snugly in strips of cloth, lying in a manger."

Suddenly, the angel was joined by a vast host of others—the armies of heaven—praising God and saying, "Glory to God in highest heaven, and peace on earth to those with whom God is pleased."

When the angels had returned to heaven, the shepherds said to each other, "Let's go to Bethlehem! Let's see this thing that has happened, which the Lord has told us about."

They hurried to the village and found Mary and Joseph. And there was the baby, lying in the manger. After seeing him, the shepherds told everyone what had happened and what the angel had said to them about this child. All who heard the shepherds' story were astonished, but Mary kept all these things in her heart and thought about them often. The shepherds went back to their flocks, glorifying and praising God for all they had heard and seen. It was just as the angel had told them.

Eight days later, when the baby was circumcised, he was named Jesus, the name given him by the angel even before he was conceived.

Then it was time for their purification offering, as required by the law of Moses after the birth of a child; so his parents took him to Jerusalem to present him to the Lord. The law of the Lord says, "If a woman's first child is a boy, he must be dedicated to the Lord." So they offered the sacrifice required in the law of the Lord—"either a pair of turtledoves or two young pigeons."

At that time there was a man in Jerusalem named Simeon. He was righteous and devout and was eagerly waiting for the Messiah to come and rescue Israel. The Holy Spirit was upon him and had revealed to him that he would not die until he had seen the Lord's Messiah. That day the Spirit led him to the Temple. So when Mary and Joseph came to present the baby Jesus to the Lord as the law required, Simeon was there. He took the child in his arms and praised God, saying,

"Sovereign Lord, now let your servant die in peace,

as you have promised.

I have seen your salvation,

which you have prepared for all people.

He is a light to reveal God to the nations,

And he is the glory of your people Israel!"

Jesus' parents were amazed at what was being said about him. Then Simeon blessed them, and he said to Mary, the baby's mother, "This child is destined to cause many in Israel to fall, and many others to rise. He has been sent as a sign from God, but many will oppose him. As a result, the deepest thoughts of many hearts will be revealed. And a sword will pierce your very soul."

Anna, a prophet, was also there in the Temple. She was the daughter of Phanuel from the tribe of Asher, and she was very old. Her husband died when they had been married only seven years. Then she lived as a widow to the age of eighty-four. She never left the Temple but stayed there day and night, worshiping God with fasting and prayer. She came along just as Simeon was talking with Mary and Joseph, and she began praising God. She talked about the child to everyone who had been waiting expectantly for God to rescue Jerusalem.

When Jesus' parents had fulfilled all the requirements of the law of the Lord, they returned home to Nazareth in Galilee. There the child grew up healthy and strong. He was filled with wisdom, and God's favor was on him.

Jesus was born in Bethlehem in Judea, during the reign of King Herod. About that time some wise men from eastern lands arrived in Jerusalem, asking, "Where is the newborn king of the Jews? We saw his star as it rose, and we have come to worship him."

King Herod was deeply disturbed when he heard this, as was everyone in Jerusalem. He called a meeting of the leading priests and teachers of religious law and asked, "Where is the Messiah supposed to be born?"

"In Bethlehem in Judea," they said, "for this is what the prophet wrote:

'And you, O Bethlehem in the land of Judah,

    are not least among the ruling cities of Judah,

for a ruler will come from you

    who will be the shepherd for my people Israel.'"

Then Herod called for a private meeting with the wise men, and he learned from them the time when the star first appeared. Then he told them, "Go to Bethlehem and search carefully for the child. And when you find him, come back and tell me so that I can go and worship him, too!"

After this interview the wise men went their way. And the star they had seen in the east guided them to Bethlehem. It went ahead of them and stopped over the place where the child was. When they saw the star, they were filled with joy! They entered the house and saw the child with his mother, Mary, and they bowed down and worshiped him. Then they opened their treasure chests and gave him gifts of gold, frankincense, and myrrh.

When it was time to leave, they returned to their own country by another route, for God had warned them in a dream not to return to Herod.

After the wise men were gone, an angel of the Lord appeared to Joseph in a dream. "Get up! Flee to Egypt with the child and his mother," the angel said. "Stay there until I tell you to return, because Herod is going to search for the child to kill him."

That night Joseph left for Egypt with the child and Mary, his mother, and they stayed there until Herod's death. This fulfilled what the Lord had spoken through the prophet: "I called my Son out of Egypt."

Herod was furious when he realized that the wise men had outwitted him. He sent soldiers to kill all the boys in and around Bethlehem who were two years old and under, based on the wise men's report of the star's first appearance. Herod's brutal action fulfilled what God had spoken through the prophet Jeremiah:

"A cry was heard in Ramah—

weeping and great mourning.

Rachel weeps for her children,

refusing to be comforted,

for they are dead."

When Herod died, an angel of the Lord appeared in a dream to Joseph in Egypt. "Get up!" the angel said. "Take the child and his mother back to the land of Israel, because those who were trying to kill the child are dead."

So Joseph got up and returned to the land of Israel with Jesus and his mother. But when he learned that the new ruler of Judea was Herod's son Archelaus, he was afraid to go there. Then, after being warned in a dream, he left for the region of Galilee. So the family went and lived in a town called Nazareth. This fulfilled what the prophets had said: "He will be called a Nazarene."

Every year Jesus' parents went to Jerusalem for the Passover festival. When Jesus was twelve years old, they attended the festival as usual. After the celebration was over, they started home to Nazareth, but Jesus stayed behind in Jerusalem. His parents didn't miss him at first, because they assumed he was among the other travelers. But when he didn't show up that evening, they started looking for him among their relatives and friends.

When they couldn't find him, they went back to Jerusalem to search for him there. Three days later they finally discovered him in the Temple, sitting among the religious teachers, listening to them and asking questions. All who heard him were amazed at his understanding and his answers.

His parents didn't know what to think. "Son," his mother said to him, "why have you done this to us? Your father and I have been frantic, searching for you everywhere."

"But why did you need to search?" he asked. "Didn't you know that I must be in my Father's house?" But they didn't understand what he meant.

Then he returned to Nazareth with them and was obedient to them. And his mother stored all these things in her heart.

Jesus grew in wisdom and in stature and in favor with God and all the people.

Then Jesus and his disciples left Jerusalem and went into the Judean countryside. Jesus spent some time with them there, baptizing people.

At this time John the Baptist was baptizing at Aenon, near Salim, because there was plenty of water there; and people kept coming to him for baptism. (This was before John was thrown into prison.) A debate broke out between John's disciples and a certain Jew over ceremonial cleansing. So John's disciples came to him and said, "Rabbi, the man you met on the other side of the Jordan River, the one you identified as the Messiah, is also baptizing people. And everybody is going to him instead of coming to us."

John replied, "No one can receive anything unless God gives it from heaven. You yourselves know how plainly I told you, 'I am not the Messiah. I am only here to prepare the way for him.' It is the bridegroom who marries the bride, and the best man is simply glad to stand with him and hear his vows. Therefore, I am filled with joy at his success. He must become greater and greater, and I must become less and less."

The Jewish leaders began harassing Jesus for breaking the Sabbath rules. But Jesus replied, "My Father is always working, and so am I." So the Jewish leaders tried all the harder to find a way to kill him. For he not only broke the Sabbath, he called God his Father, thereby making himself equal with God.

So Jesus explained, "I tell you the truth, the Son can do nothing by himself. He does only what he sees the Father doing. Whatever the Father does, the Son also does. For the Father loves the Son and shows him everything he is doing. In fact, the Father will show him how to do even greater works than healing this man. Then you will truly be astonished. For just as the Father gives life to those he raises from the dead, so the Son gives life to anyone he wants. In addition, the Father judges no one. Instead, he has given the Son absolute authority to judge, so that everyone will honor the Son, just as they honor the Father. Anyone who does not honor the Son is certainly not honoring the Father who sent him.

"I tell you the truth, those who listen to my message and believe in God who sent me have eternal life. They will never be condemned for their sins, but they have already passed from death into life.

"And I assure you that the time is coming, indeed it's here now, when the dead will hear my voice—the voice of the Son of God. And those who listen will live. The Father has life in himself, and he has granted that same life-giving power to his Son. And he has given him authority to judge everyone because he is the Son of Man. Don't be so surprised! Indeed, the time is coming when all the dead in their graves will hear the voice of God's Son, and they will rise again. Those who have done good will rise to experience eternal life, and those who have continued in evil will rise to experience judgment. I can do nothing on my own. I judge as God tells me. Therefore, my judgment is just, because I carry out the will of the one who sent me, not my own will."

John the Baptist, who was in prison, heard about all the things the Messiah was doing. So he sent his disciples to ask Jesus, "Are you the Messiah we've been expecting, or should we keep looking for someone else?"

Jesus told them, "Go back to John and tell him what you have heard and seen—the blind see, the lame walk, those with leprosy are cured, the deaf hear, the dead are raised to life, and the Good News is being preached to the poor." And he added, "God blesses those who do not fall away because of me."

As John's disciples were leaving, Jesus began talking about him to the crowds. "What kind of man did you go into the wilderness to see? Was he a weak reed, swayed by every breath of wind? Or were you expecting to see a man dressed in expensive clothes? No, people with expensive clothes live in palaces. Were you looking for a prophet? Yes, and he is more than a prophet. John is the man to whom the Scriptures refer when they say,

'Look, I am sending my messenger ahead of you,

and he will prepare your way before you.'

"I tell you the truth, of all who have ever lived, none is greater than John the Baptist. Yet even the least person in the Kingdom of Heaven is greater than he is! And from the time John the Baptist began preaching until now, the Kingdom of Heaven has been forcefully advancing, and violent people are attacking it. For before John came, all the prophets and the law of Moses looked forward to this present time. And if you are willing to accept what I say, he is Elijah, the one the prophets said would come. Anyone with ears to hear should listen and understand!"

Six days later Jesus took Peter and the two brothers, James and John, and led them up a high mountain to be alone. As the men watched, Jesus' appearance was transformed so that his face shone like the sun, and his clothes became as white as light. Suddenly, Moses and Elijah appeared and began talking with Jesus.

Peter exclaimed, "Lord, it's wonderful for us to be here! If you want, I'll make three shelters as memorials—one for you, one for Moses, and one for Elijah."

But even as he spoke, a bright cloud overshadowed them, and a voice from the cloud said, "This is my dearly loved Son, who brings me great joy. Listen to him." The disciples were terrified and fell face down on the ground.

Then Jesus came over and touched them. "Get up," he said. "Don't be afraid." And when they looked up, Moses and Elijah were gone, and they saw only Jesus.

As they went back down the mountain, Jesus commanded them, "Don't tell anyone what you have seen until the Son of Man has been raised from the dead."

Then his disciples asked him, "Why do the teachers of religious law insist that Elijah must return before the Messiah comes?"

Jesus replied, "Elijah is indeed coming first to get everything ready. But I tell you, Elijah has already come, but he wasn't recognized, and they chose to abuse him. And in the same way they will also make the Son of Man suffer." Then the disciples realized he was talking about John the Baptist.

"I tell you the truth, anyone who sneaks over the wall of a sheepfold, rather than going through the gate, must surely be a thief and a robber! But the one who enters through the gate is the shepherd of the sheep. The gatekeeper opens the gate for him, and the sheep recognize his voice and come to him. He calls his own sheep by name and leads them out. After he has gathered his own flock, he walks ahead of them, and they follow him because they know his voice. They won't follow a stranger; they will run from him because they don't know his voice."

Those who heard Jesus use this illustration didn't understand what he meant, so he explained it to them: "I tell you the truth, I am the gate for the sheep. All who came before me were thieves and robbers. But the true sheep did not listen to them. Yes, I am the gate. Those who come in through me will be saved. They will come and go freely and will find good pastures. The thief's purpose is to steal and kill and destroy. My purpose is to give them a rich and satisfying life.

"I am the good shepherd. The good shepherd sacrifices his life for the sheep. A hired hand will run when he sees a wolf coming. He will abandon the sheep because they don't belong to him and he isn't their shepherd. And so the wolf attacks them and scatters the flock. The hired hand runs away because he's working only for the money and doesn't really care about the sheep.

"I am the good shepherd; I know my own sheep, and they know me, just as my Father knows me and I know the Father. So I sacrifice my life for the sheep. I have other sheep, too, that are not in this sheepfold. I must bring them also. They will listen to my voice, and there will be one flock with one shepherd.

"The Father loves me because I sacrifice my life so I may take it back again. No one can take my life from me. I sacrifice it voluntarily. For I have the authority to lay it down when I want to and also to take it up again. For this is what my Father has commanded."

When he said these things, the people were again divided in their opinions about him. Some said, "He's demon possessed and out of his mind. Why listen to a man like that?" Others said, "This doesn't sound like a man possessed by a demon! Can a demon open the eyes of the blind?"

One day some parents brought their little children to Jesus so he could touch and bless them. But when the disciples saw this, they scolded the parents for bothering him.

Then Jesus called for the children and said to the disciples, "Let the children come to me. Don't stop them! For the Kingdom of God belongs to those who are like these children. I tell you the truth, anyone who doesn't receive the Kingdom of God like a child will never enter it."

As Jesus was going up to Jerusalem, he took the twelve disciples aside privately and told them what was going to happen to him. "Listen," he said, "we're going up to Jerusalem, where the Son of Man will be betrayed to the leading priests and the teachers of religious law. They will sentence him to die. Then they will hand him over to the Romans to be mocked, flogged with a whip, and crucified. But on the third day he will be raised from the dead."

It was nine o'clock in the morning when they crucified him. A sign announced the charge against him. It read, "The King of the Jews." Two revolutionaries were crucified with him, one on his right and one on his left.

The people passing by shouted abuse, shaking their heads in mockery. "Ha! Look at you now!" they yelled at him. "You said you were going to destroy the Temple and rebuild it in three days. Well then, save yourself and come down from the cross!"

The leading priests and teachers of religious law also mocked Jesus. "He saved others," they scoffed, "but he can't save himself! Let this Messiah, this King of Israel, come down from the cross so we can see it and believe him!" Even the men who were crucified with Jesus ridiculed him.

At noon, darkness fell across the whole land until three o'clock. Then at three o'clock Jesus called out with a loud voice, *"Eloi, Eloi, lema sabachthani?"* which means "My God, my God, why have you abandoned me?"

Some of the bystanders misunderstood and thought he was calling for the prophet Elijah. One of them ran and filled a sponge with sour wine, holding it up to him on a reed stick so he could drink. "Wait!" he said. "Let's see whether Elijah comes to take him down!"

Then Jesus uttered another loud cry and breathed his last. And the curtain in the sanctuary of the Temple was torn in two, from top to bottom.

When the Roman officer who stood facing him saw how he had died, he exclaimed, "This man truly was the Son of God!"

Very early on Sunday morning the women went to the tomb, taking the spices they had prepared. They found that the stone had been rolled away from the entrance. So they went in, but they didn't find the body of the Lord Jesus. As they stood there puzzled, two men suddenly appeared to them, clothed in dazzling robes.

The women were terrified and bowed with their faces to the ground. Then the men asked, "Why are you looking among the dead for someone who is alive? He isn't here! He is risen from the dead! Remember what he told you back in Galilee, that the Son of Man must be betrayed into the hands of sinful men and be crucified, and that he would rise again on the third day."

Then they remembered that he had said this. So they rushed back from the tomb to tell his eleven disciples—and everyone else—what had happened. It was Mary Magdalene, Joanna, Mary the mother of James, and several other women who told the apostles what had happened. But the story sounded like nonsense to the men, so they didn't believe it. However, Peter jumped up and ran to the tomb to look. Stooping, he peered in and saw the empty linen wrappings; then he went home again, wondering what had happened…

Just as they were telling about it, Jesus himself was suddenly standing there among them. "Peace be with you," he said. But the whole group was startled and frightened, thinking they were seeing a ghost!

"Why are you frightened?" he asked. "Why are your hearts filled with doubt? Look at my hands. Look at my feet. You can see that it's really me. Touch me and make sure that I am not a ghost, because ghosts don't have bodies, as you see that I do." As he spoke, he showed them his hands and his feet.

Still they stood there in disbelief, filled with joy and wonder. Then he asked them, "Do you have anything here to eat?" They gave him a piece of broiled fish, and he ate it as they watched.

Then he said, "When I was with you before, I told you that everything written about me in the law of Moses and the prophets and in the Psalms must be fulfilled." Then he opened their minds to understand the Scriptures. And he said, "Yes, it was written long ago that the Messiah would suffer and die and rise from the dead on the third day. It was also written that this message would be proclaimed in the authority of his name to all the nations, beginning in Jerusalem: 'There is forgiveness of sins for all who repent.' You are witnesses of all these things.

"And now I will send the Holy Spirit, just as my Father promised. But stay here in the city until the Holy Spirit comes and fills you with power from heaven."

Then Jesus led them to Bethany, and lifting his hands to heaven, he blessed them. While he was blessing them, he left them and was taken up to heaven. So they worshiped him and then returned to Jerusalem filled with great joy. And they spent all of their time in the Temple, praising God.

Jesus came and told his disciples, "I have been given all authority in heaven and on earth. Therefore, go and make disciples of all the nations, baptizing them in the name of the Father and the Son and the Holy Spirit. Teach these new disciples to obey all the commands I have given you. And be sure of this: I am with you always, even to the end of the age."

DECEMBER 6

SAINT NICHOLAS DAY

**Light the candle(s) according to the
corresponding week of Advent.**

Read:

Nicholas was a third-century Christian who became well known for his generosity to those in need. We would do well to mimic his posture.

God is gracious and merciful, full of love and compassion for all people. All creation looks to him to provide what is needed—and there are times when provision comes through people prompted by him to share their abundant blessings. God is honored when we give generously, joyfully, and without need for recognition.

As you commemorate Saint Nicholas, remember his love for his neighbors. He used his position in life primarily to bless others, not to make a name for himself. May your heart draw near to the Lord so that you may hear who in your life needs blessing through you.

Pray Psalm 145:8-9,14-18.
The LORD is gracious and merciful,
slow to anger and abounding in steadfast love.
The LORD is good to all,
and his compassion is over all that he has made...
The LORD upholds all who are falling,
and raises up all who are bowed down.

The eyes of all look to you,
and you give them their food in due season.
You open your hand,
satisfying the desire of every living thing.
The LORD is just in all his ways,
and kind in all his doings.
The LORD is near to all who call on him,
to all who call on him in truth.

ASK:

Whom in your life might you bless today? In what small, simple ways can you give generously?

LISTEN:

"We Labor unto Glory" by Craig Harris and Isaac Wardell

REFLECT:

Saint Nicholas Gives Alms (1685) by Jan Heinsch

December 13

SAINT LUCIA DAY

Light the candle(s) according to the
corresponding week of Advent.

Read:

Lucia of Syracuse was named appropriately—her name means "light," and tradition tells us she brought food and aid to Christians hiding in the catacombs during the reign of Diocletian. She supposedly wore candles around her head for lighting as she made her way through the caves, and she is remembered for bringing light and nourishment to those most in need.

This saint transformed her compassion into practical provision, carrying the love of God where it was needed. She also stood firm as she faced torment for aligning her choices with her faith in God, with whom she entrusted her hope. As a bringer of light, she embodied the beauty and hope we hold on to during Advent—the truth that light has come, light is coming, and light will fully come one day to bring heaven on earth.

As you commemorate Saint Lucia, remember her steadfast faith in the goodness of God, her peace in knowing that everything she owned was a gift, and her willingness to share abundantly with anyone in need. May your love for God compel you to bring light to those who need it.

Pray Psalm 112:1,4-9.

Praise the LORD!
Happy are those who fear the LORD,

who greatly delight in his commandments...
They rise in the darkness as a light for the upright;
they are gracious, merciful, and righteous.
It is well with those who deal generously and lend,
who conduct their affairs with justice.
For the righteous will never be moved;
they will be remembered forever.
They are not afraid of evil tidings;
their hearts are firm, secure in the LORD.
Their hearts are steady, they will not be afraid;
in the end they will look in triumph on their foes.
They have distributed freely, they have given to the poor;
their righteousness endures forever;
their horn is exalted in honor.

ASK:

Whom in your life might you bless today? In what ways might you encourage someone who needs a glimpse of light in the darkness?

LISTEN:

"Light of the World" by Lauren Daigle, Paul Duncan, and Paul Mabury

REFLECT:

St. Lucia (2006) by Richard Kittel

THE 12 DAYS OF CHRISTMAS

DECEMBER 25

Feast of the Nativity

This is Christmas Day, the day we celebrate the birth of Jesus Christ as Emmanuel, God with us! But *Christmastide* is a season that lasts 12 days.

Like Advent, there's no one right way to commemorate these 12 days—but after 4 weeks of waiting expectantly, it's a delight to finally celebrate Christmas. So watch movies, enjoy outings, bake, drink, and feast. Keep your decorations up through January 5. You've waited and waited—there's no reason to quickly pack up the season.

Here's a summary of some of the other feast or commemorative days recognized during (and immediately following) the 12 days of Christmas.

DECEMBER 26

Feast of Saint Stephen

Stephen is considered one of the first deacons of the Church, anointed to minister to widows on behalf of Jesus's apostles (Acts 6:1-6). He was also the first martyr;

he was stoned to death as Saul (later Paul) oversaw the ordeal (7:54-60). Stephen proclaimed the gospel, and during his stoning he saw a vision of Jesus standing at God's right hand.

DECEMBER 27
Feast of Saint John

John was the "beloved disciple" and a good friend of Jesus. After journeying through the season of Advent, walking from darkness to light, it's good to remember John—who, according to tradition, wrote the Gospel of John, which emphasizes Christ's incarnation and describes him as light infiltrating a dark world.

DECEMBER 28
Feast of the Holy Innocents

This somber day commemorates the innocent children killed by Herod in Bethlehem as he attempted to eliminate the young Messiah (Matthew 2:16-18). As we remember these innocent children, we also remember all innocents subject to violence around the world.

JANUARY 1
Feast of the Holy Name

On this day, we remember when Jesus was circumcised on the eighth day and, in keeping with Jewish custom, was given his name (Luke 2:21). Both Mary and Joseph were told to name their baby Jesus (Luke 1:31; Matthew 1:21), which means "God saves." We commemorate the name of Jesus on this day because of God's power to save in Jesus's name.

JANUARY 5

Eve of the Epiphany

Also called "Twelfth Night," this is the last day of Christmas and the day before Epiphany. Historically, feasts and evening parties were held on this day throughout villages (and many cultures still hold these traditions presently). During these parties, roles in society were often reversed, with servants being served by the nobles. Sometimes a coin or dried bean was baked into a rich king's cake, and whoever found the coin or bean in their slice was lord or lady of the evening.

Today, January 5 is still a fantastic excuse for hosting an evening party with friends to celebrate the finale of Christmastide.

JANUARY 6

Feast of the Epiphany

Epiphany, the feast commemorating the arrival of the Magi to Jesus, follows the 12 days of Christmastide. These wise men were not Jews, and though we don't know exactly why they were looking for the Jewish Messiah, we read that they were led to him by the light of a star (Matthew 2:1-11). Their arrival reminds us that Christ's Incarnation is for the whole world and that we can all find him when we follow the light.

This is a common day for taking down Christmas decorations and cleaning out some of the clutter. It's also a good day to pray a blessing over your house for the coming year, asking God to make your home a haven for all who enter. Just as Christ came to dwell with us, you can pray that those who walk through your door find Christ at home with you and invite him to be at home in their own lives.

ADVENT DATES

First Sunday of Advent 2020: November 29

First Sunday of Advent 2021: November 28

First Sunday of Advent 2022: November 27

First Sunday of Advent 2023: December 3

First Sunday of Advent 2024: December 1

First Sunday of Advent 2025: November 30

First Sunday of Advent 2026: November 29

First Sunday of Advent 2027: November 28

First Sunday of Advent 2028: December 3

First Sunday of Advent 2029: December 2

First Sunday of Advent 2030: December 1

NOTES

[1]Dietrich Bonhoeffer to Maria von Wedemeyer, December 13, 1943, in Dietrich Bonhoeffer, *God Is in the Manger: Reflections on Advent and Christmas* (Louisville, KY: Westminster John Knox Press, 2012), 5.

[2]William P. Saunders, "What Is the Liturgical Year?" *Catholic Straight Answers*, accessed December 11, 2019, http://catholicstraightanswers.com/what-is-the-liturgical-year.

[3]Saunders, "What Is the Liturgical Year?"

[4]Joan Chittister, *A Monastery Almanac* (Erie, PA: Benetvision, 2010), quoted in "Prepare Your Heart, Advent Begins Dec. 2," November 27, 2018, http://www.joanchittister.org/word-from-joan/11-27-2018/prepare-your-heart-advent-begins-dec-2.

[5]Michelle Blake, *The Tentmaker* (New York: Penguin Putnam, 1999), 155.

[6]Óscar Romero, *The Violence of Love*, comp. and trans. James R. Brockman (Maryknoll, NY: Orbis, 2004), 107.

[7]Luci Shaw, "Third Sunday of Advent," *God with Us: Rediscovering the Meaning of Christmas*, ed. Greg Pennoyer (Brewster, MA: Paraclete, 2007), 77.

[8]Renzo Allegri, "Mother Teresa's Christmas," Messenger of Saint Anthony, May 3, 2003, https://www.messengersaintanthony.com/content/mother-teresas-christmas.

[9]Dorothy Sayers, *Christian Letters to a Post-Christian World*, ed. Roderick Jellema (Grand Rapids, MI: Eerdmans, 1969), 14.

[10]Hamilton Wright Mabie, *My Study Fire* (New York: Dodd, Mead and Company, 1900), 54.

[11]Thomas Merton, *Raids on the Unspeakable* (New York: New Directions, 1966), 72.

PERSONAL REFLECTION

ACKNOWLEDGMENTS

First, thank you to Kyle, Tate, Reed, and Finn. Rolling our clumsy beeswax candles, cramming them into an unimpressive log, and reading from Scripture by flickering candlelight will always be my favorite holiday tradition of ours. You're the best I could ever hope for, and I remain astonished at my good fortune to call you family.

Thank you to Caroline TeSelle for your tireless help, support, encouragement, and, most of all, friendship. "Assistant" seems like such a small word to describe you. "Armor-bearer" is more like it. I'm also grateful for the work, camaraderie, and advocacy of my literary agent and friend, Jenni Burke.

I'm grateful for friends and their support, far and wide, whether it's working alongside you in the trenches or clinking glasses during happy hour: Beth, Emily, Myquillyn, Kendra, Seth, Haley, Erin, Sarah, Shawn, Alia, Bethany, Crystal, Katherine, Christine, Andrea, Lisa, Paul, Katie, Shaun, Meena, Jason, and all names of those I've forgotten, always the most terrifying prospect of writing any published book save for missing a typo. Thanks so much to all the readers who support my work through Books & Crannies. And thanks to Father Peter and Father Nick for your pastoral leadership and encouragement.

I'm always happy when I find professional partnerships a source of fun, and working with Kathleen Kerr as editor is no exception here. From pastries at the Hideaway to now, it's been a pleasure. Thanks, also, to the good people at Harvest House who made this work possible: Jessica, Kim, Shann, Sherrie, Brad, and beyond. And of course, thanks to Caleb Peavy for his tireless work.

Finally, I'm grateful for all the artists whose work draws me closer to God during Advent, from the nameless monk in the Middle Ages to Leslie Odom Jr; from Russian iconographers during the Renaissance to the modern-day graphic artist. The world is lovelier because of you.

ABOUT THE AUTHOR

Tsh Oxenreider is the bestselling author of several books, most notably *At Home in the World*, her memoir about her family's year traveling around the world and living out of backpacks. She's also a travel guide, teacher, and top-ranked podcaster, and she lives in Georgetown, Texas, with her husband and three children. She is equally happy putzing around her backyard, snorkeling the Great Barrier Reef with her family, and standing in line for cheap Broadway tickets in chilly New York City with her teenage daughter. You can find Tsh online at tshoxenreider.com.